To Bonni
    Now a

Save the stories of your
fabulous life! I hope
you enjoy mine!
            Dawn

Saving Our Lives

Volume Two

Essays to Release
the Writer
in *YOU*

D. Margaret Hoffman

D. Margaret Hoffman
Berlin, CT
Jan. 7, 2018

Davanti &
Vine Press

Cover Design: GoOnWrite.com
Format: Polgarus Studios

ISBN: 978-0-9979169-0-4 (paperback)
ISBN: 978-0-9979169-1-1 (e-book)

Davanti &
Vine Press
www.davantiandvinepress.com

For My Family
Because You Make My Life Worth Saving

"Once something is written, it *stays* written,
reaching across time. Forever."
Saving Our Lives,
Volume One

Table of Contents

Introduction—Welcome to Volume Two 1

    I Could Write a Book 3

    Saving the Life That You're Saving................................... 8

Part One—Preferences and Predilections.......................... 13

    Shopping for Shapewear: Confessions of a Girdle Girl .. 15

    All's Vanity 20

    If You're Never Fully Dressed Without a Manicure,

    Then I've Been Naked All My Life.................................. 28

    MP3 Flashback 38

    Fridge Detective.. 47

Part Two—Mistakes Were Made.................................... 55

    What The Little One Saw 57

    GOT 'EM!... 65

    The Wine Shrine... 72

Part Three—Woodpecker Wars.. 85

    Episode One—*He Is Not Afraid Of Me* 87

    Episode Two—*Brain Size Is Not a Factor* 95

    Episode Three—*So This Is How It Ends*

    (With Apologies to Edgar Allan Poe)............................ 104

Part Four—You *Can* Get There From Here 113

    Caped Crusader 115

    The Wonder Horse of Saskatoon 123

    Olive Tree, Very Pretty 132

    And the Birds Still Sing 137

    How to Pack: A Primer for the Organizationally

    Challenged 153

Part Five—Spring Forward, Fall Back 165

    Winter's Last Hurrah or We Dare the Ides of March ... 167

    The Rights of Spring 174

    Oh, My Achin' April 183

Part Six—Life's Lessons 191

    The Girl Who Sang 193

    Maycomb, McKinley Drive and Me 202

    What Teachers Do 209

    The Sycamore 214

    Both Sides Now 220

    When a Writing Teacher Becomes a Teaching Writer

    or It's About Time I Learned My Lesson 227

    Thanks, Shirley! 236

Part Seven—Musings 241

    Educide 243

    Untitled 253

    One of a Kind 263

    Phased 270

    It's Time 276

Afterword—I Have a Great Idea! Now What?................ 281

Acknowledgments... 291
About the Author 295

Introduction
Welcome to Volume Two

If you have read Volume One of this series, *Saving Our Lives: Essays to Inspire the Writer in YOU*, welcome back. I'm thrilled that you are along for another ride. If you have not yet read Volume One, please know that Volume Two of the series, *Saving Our Lives: Essays to Release the Writer in YOU*, can be enjoyed on its own. Volume One contains more essays to engage readers and lots of advice to motivate writers. I hope you will seek it out. But, while the books are companions to one another, they are, like the partners of any healthy couple, capable of facing the world alone when they have to. Still, they tend to bring out the best in each other, so I hope you will consider collecting the set.

Volume One reveals my fondness for the small notebook, the single idea and the mission to save our lives. With the written word as our instrument, we can, at whatever level we choose, compose the stories of our lives one small idea, memory, observation, opinion or rant at a time. I am never without a 3½ x 5½ Moleskine-brand hardcover notebook and a Pilot G2 #5 fine point pen. When something strikes me that I want to remember, I can capture it—on the spot. It doesn't take very much time or effort. Open. Jot. Close. Done. Memory saved. Forever.

And once a thought is saved, there are all kinds of things that we can do with it.

I weave mine into personal essays. You might do the same with yours, or you might write stories or plays or songs or poems instead. You could even leave those original jottings just as they are, satisfied that your growing collection of little notebooks will serve as a respectable chronicle of your life.

It's your life, so it's your call.

Volume Two, like its significant other, is a collection of essays born from the idea that our life experiences don't have to be life-altering to have value. Many of the essays in this book originally appeared as posts on my blog site and others are meeting readers here for the first time. All are followed by lists of prompts that will help readers to relate personally to my experiences and will inspire writers to save their lives the way I am saving mine. I hope that you will interact with these essays in ways that will make them meaningful and encouraging for you—as a reader, as a writer and as the caretaker of a life worth saving.

I Could Write a Book

I wish I had a book sale for every time I've heard someone say, "My life is crazy! I could write a book!" But I suppose I'd have to refund the money for everyone who's said it and then didn't do it—which is just about everyone I've ever heard say it.

So, then, you might say, if people whose lives are fraught with drama don't get it done, what hope is there for me? My life is so ordinary. Nothing interesting ever happens to me. What is there worth writing about?

Well, let's see.

In Volume One of this series (*Saving Our Lives: Essays to Inspire the Writer in YOU*), you read essays about some pretty everyday stuff. Sure, there were some big life events represented—weddings, funerals, trips of a lifetime. But there were also essays about days at the beach, lost cats, dead plants and toilet paper. And then there were others about sports aversions, nightmares, dress shopping and broken air conditioners. In Volume Two, prepare to be amazed as you read about, among other things, concert ticket troubles, wayward woodpeckers, fourth-grade divas, fridge magnets and girdles.

What is all this stuff? I'll tell you what it is. *It's life.* And it's happening to all of us every minute of every day. It is this culmination of personal experience that makes us one of the crowd *and* one of a kind—routine *and* exceptional, familiar *and* mysterious, universal *and* unique. The diva is in the details. While the experiences might be communal, the details are exclusively yours.

What could be more exciting than capturing the living, breathing reality of a life as it is lived? And what life do you know more about than any other? Exactly. And all of it will slip away if you don't catch it—and save it.

And why should you? Because it's important.

Let me explain.

• *It's important to you.*

Writing anything down gives ideas a body. Things that float nebulously in your head suddenly have shape and form. You can see them, touch them, watch them grow. You can look at the accumulation of words to see what you've done. It's like making a list. I might have done a respectable amount of work in a day, but it always feels like I accomplished more when I see items written down and checked off a list. Likewise, you may think your life is ordinary until you see the truth of it appearing page by page. You are much more interesting than you think you are. Don't confuse "everyday" with "ordinary." The two are not synonymous. You have a life full of stories worth saving—how you do your job, how you get dinner on the table, how you managed a difficult relationship, how you bought your first car, how you get through the day, how you get through the night, how you *live.* Your experiences have value. Sometimes all it takes is seeing them written down to drive that point home

• *It's important to people who would benefit from your insights.*

You know stuff. Just being alive, going to school, making a living, raising a family, solving problems and getting through the night provides you with experiences that others may find instructional or fun or (dare I say it?) *interesting.* Someone *will* want to read about what you know. You never know how your words will affect people, teach them, comfort them, light a fire under them. I learned this lesson from years of teaching. You never know whose life will be touched by what you have to say. Unless, of course, you never say it. Then the answer is, "No one's."

• *It's important to the integrity of your story.*

The oral tradition of storytelling is sketchy at best these days and depending on others to remember your story and get it right is a dangerous proposition. Remember the kids' game called "Gossip"? I whisper something into your ear. You whisper what you heard into the next person's ear and so on down the line. When the last person reveals what he or she heard, most of the time it bears no earthly resemblance to the original. So go our life stories. Lovely stories, juicy stories, sad stories will morph into the unrecognizable or disappear altogether. But, as I have said a zillion times, writing stays. It has authority. Your written-down version of a story, presumably the truth, will trump the spoken account every time. It will *become* the story—straight from the horse's mouth. That makes it the only one worth knowing.

• *It's important to the future.*

Think of it this way. Have you ever wished you could reach back into the past and ask an ancestor what his or her life was like? Have you ever wondered what your great-great grandparents thought about things, how they got through the day, what they loved, what vexed them? Have you ever wondered whether or not you're like them, how they paved the way for you, what advice they might give you? Ever wish you could sit down and talk with them to get some perspective on their world in an attempt to figure out your own?

Me, too. I have a thousand questions I'd ask them. Unfortunately, I'll never have the opportunity. The past is gone, and along with it has gone all of the accumulated knowledge, insight and experience of all of the generations of my family that preceded me. How sad this is to me. How profoundly sad.

I can't reach back. But I can reach forward. So can you. We can touch the future simply by saving our lives now—for them. In whatever small way we can. Imagine finding your great-great grandmother's writings. What a thrill that would be.

Now, imagine your great-great grandchildren finding yours.

It can only happen if you save it for them now. It's worth it.

You're worth it.

Do it.

There are so many reasons for doing this—personal, cultural, historical. When I watch historical documentary films, for instance, the ones that make the biggest impact on me are those that take their content from diaries and journals and the lives of actual people. Ken Burns, master documentary filmmaker, knew this early in his career. Just watch any portion of his magnum opus *The Civil War* to be immediately pulled into the events not through statistics or strategies or policies (though all of these things are present) but through the lives of the "everyday" people who lived it.

And how do we know about these lives? Letters, diaries, journals, personal essays—the written records not of professional writers or journalists or politicians, but of boys writing home to their mothers, husbands writing their desperate, final words home to their wives, women keeping diaries as they struggled to maintain their homes and raise their children alone. Farmers, teachers, soldiers, doctors. People writing. Is there anything more permanent?

These people didn't set out to create historical documents. But that's what happened. They unintentionally saved their own lives—and enriched ours. Their words live among us, even now, and will still be here when we are gone.

And, so, it's time for us, too, to pay it forward.

"I could write a book," you say. Yes, you could, on whatever scale you choose. Write to your great-great grandchildren what you wish your great-great grandparents wrote to you. It's a chance to reach out to the future. To become a part of history. To be immortal.

Do it.

Saving the Life That You're Saving

So, you've decided to give it a try. You've bought yourself a copy of *Saving Our Lives*, a 3½ X 5 ½ Moleskine notebook and a blue Pilot G2 #5 gel pen (or whatever else you like to write in and with). Each time you sit down to read an essay in *Saving Our Lives,* you choose a prompt from the bulleted list at the end and explore your own experiences on this topic by making notes in your Moleskine. Sometimes you stick to the prompt and other times you wander at will into new territory. The pages are filling up like crazy. You like this.

Now what?

Here are some ideas for saving the life that you're saving.

• *Leave it just as it is.*

Ultimately, this whole activity is just for you. Your notebook can be a place to store stuff, like a sock drawer. When you need a sock, you open the drawer, get one out (or maybe two) and put it on. Likewise, when you need a story to share, or when you just feel like reminiscing, you skim through the pages of your notebook, pull out a story and tell it to someone or just think about it and smile. Make tea.

- *Write a letter.*

If your response to a prompt reminds you of someone, turn it into a letter (preferably on paper) and send it. Hopefully, you'll get a reply and the written record of a relationship is born. If that person is deceased or otherwise inaccessible, write the letter anyway. Perhaps you could write the reply that you imagine the recipient might have written back to you. If this continues, it could turn into something very interesting.

- *Make quick notes.*

Jot stories on sticky notes and tuck them in birthday cards, thank you notes, get-wells, thinking of you cards, etc. They can start with things like, "Do you remember the time…?" "I'll bet you didn't know this!" "When you were small…" "How's this for crazy?" "I've never told this to anyone…" "When I was your age…" "Here's something I haven't thought about in a long time." "Thought you might be interested to know…" "I was young once, too." (Email these if you must, but they make a more dramatic statement when they come in the actual USPS mail.)

- *Compose and send the best holiday letter ever!*

- *Start a "Saving Our Lives" exchange.*

Share one of your responses at the next gathering of family and/or friends and encourage others to do the same. Each night at the dinner table or each time a particular group gathers, a different person can be in charge of starting the conversation with a snippet or a story saved from his or her life. You are in charge. Set a good example by always being ready to go if someone else forgets. They'll catch on.

• *Write an essay.*

When a memory strikes a chord, write its story in full detail—as an essay, like mine. Just start telling the story and don't stop until it's finished. You might be surprised to discover how satisfying this is.

• *Write a song or a poem.*

There are lots of ways to tell your stories. The genre is up to you.

• *Get fictional.*

Short stories and plays take events and impose a certain structure upon them. You may need to adjust the facts to make them fit. But this is not to say that your life events have to be expressed just the way they happened. Some writers say that the only way they can tell the truth is through the writing of fiction. Let your life events be the springboard for a story or play and then make things turn out any way you want them to!

• *Make gift folders.*

An essay (or song or story or poem or short play), given to the right person in a decorative folder or printed as a booklet with a photo or two, can be a cherished and personal gift. You might consider writing at least a portion of it by hand.

• *Start a binder.*

If you are writing your stories as essays or letters, get a nice, fat, five-inch three-ring binder in which to store them. It's fun to watch it fill up. You will notice before too long, that you are actually writing a book.

• *Make gift binders.*

If you have a collection of essays completed, print them and give them out as gifts. If you are older, make sure that they go to young people. That is, after all, how this whole "touching the future" thing works.

• *Start a blog.*

Blogs can be as public or as private as you want to make them. There are many vehicles for this as an online search will show. My first blog was a free one on Wordpress.com, a user-friendly site that served me well. But don't take blogging lightly. A blog is a commitment, even if it's just for you, so, once you set one up, make a pact with yourself to contribute to it regularly. If you allow readers in, this is essential.

• *Write a book.*

This is not for the faint of heart. You can take it from me; it's harder than it looks. But it can be done. You can take that from me, too.

The point is that what you do with your notes—how you develop them, how you share them, how you decorate them—is all up to you. This can be as big or as small of a project as you want to make it. A committed effort of any magnitude will be effective and meaningful and welcomed.

To me, there are two important facets to this process. First, you must see the value in your opinions and experiences, whatever they are. Your life skills, activities, health issues, travels, life choices—they matter and should be preserved. You live your life the way you do for a reason—because of choices you've made, because of successes and failures you've experienced, because of genes you've inherited. You see life from a place that is all your own. Someone *will* want to know.

Second, you must see your worth as a writer. Writing is the most efficient, most permanent and most satisfying way to save your life. You don't have to be a fine writer to get your ideas down on paper. If you decide to publish, there are people out there who can help you with that. But the ideas and the expression of them—this is the unique part. This *has* to come from you. If you don't write it down, in words that *you* have chosen, your life will be left for others to interpret or, worse, it will go unsaved altogether, like the lives of most of my ancestors and, I would venture to guess, many of yours.

How you choose to do this is up to you. If you'd like to add to my list of suggestions, please send me an email and I'll include your contributions in the third volume of *Saving Our Lives* and/or on my blog.

Do it.

You can.

And you should.

Part One
Preferences and Predilections

We live in a tell-all world. Reality TV, social media and round-the-clock connectedness have created a level of scrutiny that was, at first, frightening and intrusive. But there is an upside. The more we share about our lives, the more we realize that we are all more alike than we ever knew. And when we admit that our own personal oddities are not that odd after all, that they are part of being human and that they have value, then we become more willing to acknowledge them, reveal them and, dare I say, even save them for others to learn from and enjoy.

Those of us who keep blogs and write essays believe that we are representative samples of the world in which we live. Our ideas and our experiences, our beliefs and our longings, our quirks and our peccadilloes all emerge from the same place as everyone else's and, as such, we assume that expressing them will not only be liberating for us, but also supportive or entertaining or inspirational or cathartic for someone else. So we look hard at our preferences and predilections, we find words to describe them and we hope that others will be encouraged to do the same.

To that end, Volume Two of *Saving Our Lives* begins with essays that delve into the little issues of life that confront us and reveal us as we are. For me, some of these issues involve coming to terms with modern technology, discovering the artistry of the French gel manicure, facing my fears of foundational undergarments and revealing at last my long-held theory of the revelatory powers of the refrigerator door.

Welcome to my world. I'll bet it's a lot like yours.

Shopping for Shapewear: Confessions of a Girdle Girl

Technology is a generational thing. The older I get, the more new trends there are to assimilate. I try to keep up with the times, but I do tend to fall into patterns that are comfortable and predictable. It makes me feel like I have a modicum of control and gives me an excuse not to navigate the overwhelming world of the newfangled. But I'm not talking about laptops, digital cameras or smartphones. I'm good with all that. I'm talking about underwear.

My recent initiation into the tangled jungle of "shapewear" began innocently enough. I was going to a wedding and wanted something foundational to wear under a new dress. I ran into Kohl's, expecting to grab something slimming, try it on and go. My previous experience with modern shapewear was a pair of compression running shorts that I bought at a sporting goods store in about ten minutes and wore all summer under dresses. I didn't wear them as slimmers. I wore them because they suddenly made wearing dresses in summer comfortable, cooler than capris and less repulsive than shorts. They probably would have worked just fine for the wedding, but I don't get dressed up very much anymore, so I wanted the real deal.

I shop at Kohl's often and had walked past this department a million times. From a distance, the garments looked harmless enough. They were, I thought, just variations on a theme.

But then, I stepped inside.

If this were a movie, the shot would be me turning in a circle in one direction while the camera circled around me the opposite way. My head would be jerking from right to left and my arms would flail and the background would blur and close-up shots of unrecognizable undergarments would be intercut with shots of my panicked face. Squealing, staccato violins would provide the soundtrack. Eisenstein would direct. Or Hitchcock.

How could I, a grown woman who has worn underwear her whole life, be so out of touch with the current state of intimate apparel? Where were the slips? How do you get into that? How do you get out of this? Does that come with a whip? Do you just *not* go to the bathroom? Or sit? And, *where are the slips?*

*****

When I was a kid, my mother would go to Sears, walk up to a table, flip through boxes that said Maidenform or Playtex, and pull out one long-line bra and one girdle. Done. I assume at one time or another she needed to try them on or be fitted or something, but I never saw this happen. More likely she took her measurements at home, behind closed doors, and then matched them to the measurements on the box. The bra was white and had bony stays up the sides, like a cage, for firm support and lift. The girdle had an embroidered panel in the front that could probably stop bullets. I realize now that when I hugged her, I was never really hugging *her.* Under her housedress was a fortress.

My first girdle was a short-lived thing, exciting to me mostly because it was meant to hold up my first pairs of nylons, a true rite of passage in those days. I was willing to tolerate the rolling up of the legs and the pinching of the garters because that was what girls did to grow up. Besides I was already painfully aware of the pudge that was my middle and I was happy to have help sucking it in.

But we were on the brink of a paradigm shift that would change womanhood and the fashion industry as we knew it.

Let's hear it for—Pantyhose!

And once someone had the brilliant idea to put the girdle into the pantyhose and call them "control tops," we never looked back. The word "girdle" fell out of our vocabulary, never to be uttered again, unless we were talking about our mothers.

And that's where I got stuck on the lingerie roller coaster. 1970. Pantyhose have come a long way since then, sure, but they are still pantyhose—understandable, manageable, comfortable, modern, inexpensive, fashionable. So much better than girdles and garters and so much simpler than shapewear. Pantyhose under slacks. Pantyhose and a half-slip under dresses and skirts. This is what makes sense to me. Why do we need anything else?

And where have I been for years as the market changed around me? In J. C. Penney's buying the same bras and half-slips that I've been wearing *forever*. In Target buying Hanes Hi-Cut briefs in packages of six. In CVS, buying control-top pantyhose in assorted shades of beige and black. Obviously not here in the Shapewear Department of Kohl's trying to figure out what won't hurt me.

*****

Not to be intimidated by this labyrinth of spandex, I gathered my wits and a few random "body shapers"—firmers, torsettes, cinchers, open bust body suits, and, for laughs, a high-waist body thong—and marched into the dressing room. Such wriggling you can't imagine! It was exhausting. Liposuction would have been easier. I try to stay in shape, but dancing with these boa constrictors stirred up muscle groups that really preferred to be left alone. Department store lingerie, circa 1970, was looking pretty good.

I bought an all-over shaper that looks like a black tank dress for Jessica Rabbit. It cost somewhere around $60.00. I never wore it. But I take it out to look at from time to time—as a reminder of how hip and modern I am. Then I tug on a pair of control-top pantyhose, check the mirror to make sure that my slip isn't showing and go out to face the world.

Saving *Your* Life

- Why do we put ourselves through the agony of wearing foundational undergarments? Write about your body image and what it compels you to do.

- What's the last thing that made you feel out of touch with the times?

- Think of something that you use now that didn't exist when you were growing up. (For me, this would include things like laptops or crock pots or microwaves or pocket calculators or remote controls.) Write about how you got things done without it.

- Write about something that you wore or used for the first time that marked the end of your childhood.

- What one thing about adults did you envy as a kid?

- Write about a classic item from your youth that you wish you still had.

- What do you own that you've never used? Why'd you buy it? Why'd you keep it?

- What old-fashioned way of doing things do you refuse to give up? Why?

- Trace how one item or way of doing something has "improved" over the course of your life. Do *you* see it as an improvement?

- Did anything else about this essay remind you of your own experiences? In your notebook, jot down one memory, thought or opinion that popped into your head as you were reading.

All's Vanity

If you know me, you know that I am a lover of paper. I take pleasure in the feel of a book and the smell of a library, especially an old one. I read a print newspaper every day and I love to get mail.

Yet, when I write, I no longer compose in longhand. Instead I use a keyboard and a screen and I distribute my work as blog posts and emails and texts and e-books. Still, I'm much happier navigating the hard copy of a book than the cyber one—flipping back and forth, rereading passages, making notes in the margins, crimping corners—and it's fun to find creative ways to mark my place with everything from an elegant silk ribbon to a tattered picture of my kids to the price tag from my new blouse to a strand of hair from my pillow or a piece of thread from my hem. Yet, I am steadily filling my e-reader with books that are easy to see in the dark and balance in bed and take with me wherever I go. I can make the print enormous. I can change the color of the page. I can get a new book with a click. Instantly. Even in the middle of the night.

Then I can ask it to read me to sleep.

Technology has its merits. But every time I think I'm just going to give in to it, I pick up something in print that blows me away and I realize that, while I will use and appreciate digital technology, I will never abandon print. Ever.

I cannot lie. I am a bi-bibliophile. I like it both ways.

Old and new technologies don't have to be mutually exclusive. There are lots of ways that they co-exist in our lives. You may think, for instance, that silent movies are a thing of the past, but their techniques are alive and well in modern filmmaking. Whenever you watch a montage scene where the music plays under shots that are edited together to show a kid growing up or a relationship blossoming into a love affair or a bunch of Italian guys suiting up for a massacre while a baptism is going on, you are watching the marriage of silent film with sound. One hasn't usurped the other. Instead, you get both at once.

Likewise, TV didn't wipe out the film industry. Each found ways to adjust to the other's existence. Color photography didn't replace the brooding shadows of black and white. But now we can choose which better suits our subject. Cars are a necessity, but people still ride bicycles. And horses. We love our microwaves. They sit right next to our conventional ovens. Electric lights cut through the darkness, but who doesn't have a drawer full of candles in the house somewhere? It's convenient to fly to faraway places, but sometimes it's nice to board a ship and cruise there instead. We can listen to music twenty-four hours a day on a host of devices, but people still go to live concerts, the same as they did in Mozart's time. I have an air conditioner *and* a fan, a furnace *and* a fireplace. I didn't throw away my needles when I bought a sewing machine, I didn't burn all my pencils when I got my laptop and I didn't stop reading paper books when I got an e-reader.

There *are* things, of course, that outlive their usefulness and disappear, like manual typewriters and eight-track tape decks and Pong and big hair. I am wistful, perhaps, but not mournful of their passing. Their real jobs were to pave the way for something better. Print, like fireplaces and candles and needles and horses, will find a way to adapt to the onslaught of technology and it will adjust to changing times. It still serves an inimitable purpose. Print and digital products will learn how to coexist and will settle into their appropriate niches as time goes on.

I was not always so sure of this. But I am now. How do I know? It comes down, quite simply, to a tale of two subscriptions.

*****

Being bi, I have experimented extensively with different reading methods to discover what works for me. My e-reader is great for bestsellers, romance novels and books that I am likely to read only once. It's also a good place for samples of authors and genres that are new to me, books without illustrations (although my e-reader model has a vivid color display), essays, short fiction, anything I must have this very minute, books with which I plan to travel and books that are too expensive to buy in print.

There is no negotiating the fact that I will buy a print version of the work of any author I am likely to meet so that I can have it signed. I will buy a print version of any book that I would like to loan to someone. I will usually opt for a print version of a modern play and nothing but print for Shakespeare. Anything that I need to study or analyze must be in print. For me nothing can emulate the effectiveness of underlining by hand and making actual notes in actual margins. And I like to donate used books to my local library for their on-going book sale, so I keep that in mind when deciding on a format for my next literary purchase.

Most of these reasons for going print, I know, are pure preference and are not enough to insure that print will find its place in future generations. Technical things like formatting and illustration display and even loaning a book to someone or having it signed are all things that can be done digitally and most likely will be commonplace sooner than I think.

I am confident, though, that print books, like silent movie techniques and black and white photography and live music, will survive.

I know this because I read *Vanity Fair*.

*****

I recently took out two new magazine subscriptions. Many print subscriptions that I already have and even my daily newspaper have a dot-com component with more stories online, but I rarely access them. My bi-bibliophilia is one thing. My late-onset ADD is another and bouncing back and forth from magazine to screen is distracting and stressful. I find no pleasure in it. But some print subscriptions also come with an online version of the magazine itself and that I can do. While I prefer a print magazine, I can do a digital one in a pinch and I can see how people brought up with this technology could find the modern version preferable.

When I was offered a good deal on a digital subscription of *Family Circle* magazine, I took it. It is my first 100% digital subscription. I like it. I can swipe the screen and the corner of the display curls up like a real page turning. I can make all pages appear in thumbnail at the bottom of the screen or I can make the thumbnails fill the screen so that I can tap and jump to any page I want at any time. I can tap again and switch from a magazine view to a text view that is plainer and easier to read. A cover shows up in my gallery every time a new issue is published and the older ones are stored in my device for easy access anytime. On my e-reader, the images are sharp, the colors are vibrant and the touchscreen is responsive so this digital reading experience is the closest I have ever come to feeling like I have the real magazine in my hands. Of course, I still can't cut out the recipes or draw moustaches on the models or make collages out of the pages or roll the whole thing up when I need to swat at a mosquito. These are drawbacks, to be sure, but I'll adjust.

I admit that I do enjoy the novelty and the convenience of my *Family Circle* subscription. It makes it clear to me that digital reading is here to stay. But it is my second new magazine subscription that gives me hope for the future of print.

I've always enjoyed leafing through *Vanity Fair* magazine in the library and I would pick it up on the newsstand from time to time—usually when Johnny Depp was on the cover. But I never afforded myself the luxury of a subscription until recently. I really love its heft and its glossy, New York, big-time feel. Sitting down with the November, January and February issues (did December get tossed out with the remains of Christmas?) satisfied my need for tangible reading in a thousand ways. The arrival of each issue has become an event worthy of a warm fire, a homemade afghan and a hot cup of tea.

I love everything about this magazine—the photography, the classy mix of high fashion and eclectic reading, the ads, the perfume samples, even the cardstock inserts that, in other magazines, I usually can't throw away fast enough. Nothing in

VF deserves to be overlooked. It is a magazine with which one must take one's time—maybe two sittings, maybe more. It's a guilty pleasure with an intellectual inclination and an aesthetic flair. It cries out to be treated with respect, to be held in your hands, even, perhaps, to be given its own bookmark and a place of honor on the coffee table. This is not your mother's grocery store check-out line magazine.

And I felt this way even before the massive March issue hit my mailbox.

Thicker than November, January and February combined, this particular March issue is three hundred and seventy-six pages long. The Table of Contents doesn't appear until page fifty-two. It continues on page seventy and finishes on page ninety and the masthead doesn't arrive at the party until page ninety-eight. In between, the pages are filled with beautifully photographed models wearing designer clothes I love to look at but could never wear. Rail-thin, pensive and often shot from low angles, these models have stories in their faces, the kind that tempt the teacher in me to tear the pictures from the binding and hand them out to neophyte novelists in search of inspiration. On page one hundred and one, I am offered the opportunity to receive *VF* as a monthly download on my tablet or iPhone. I take it, but it makes me sad for those who believe that it is possible to truly experience these photographs in digitized miniature.

Just think of all of the novels that will never be written.

But the sensory experience of March goes far beyond the visual. The perfume samples—Prada, Michael Kors, Ralph Lauren—create a world that feels real, so real you can smell it. The paper itself is of varying weights and thicknesses and there are several fold-out sections, making the material on the page stand out not just to your eyes, but to your fingers. Because of them, the magazine falls in sections when you fan the pages with your thumb, creating distinct sounds as they land. If you were blind, you could navigate this magazine through touch and smell and sound.

It's amazing really.

So modern.

There are many aspects of *Vanity Fair* that I'm sure I could enjoy on my e-reader. The glorious full-page, suitable-for-pinning-up-in-my-laundry-room photographs of movie stars, staples of the Annual March Hollywood Post-Oscar Issue, are not among them. Nor are the striking Vera Wang models or the multiple full pages of text, sequential and triple-columned and narrow-margined and fabulous. On a screen, it's a visual experience, to be sure. But, on paper, it's a sensory feast.

Vanity Fair is a magazine that understands the power of paper. But it also understands the tide of its times and so it is, by necessity, bi-bibliophilic. Like me. And that's OK.

It's good to have it both ways.

Saving *Your* Life

- What do your magazine subscriptions say about you? Make a list of all the subscriptions you can remember having in your life. Does a picture of you emerge?

- Do you own an e-reader? If so, what do you see as its strengths and weaknesses? If not, why not?

- Write about your very favorite magazine. What, to you, are its most attractive features? Do you read it differently than other magazines?

- Do you prefer the digital or paper version? Why?

- How do you deal with reading in the digital age? What are your preferences? What are your objections?

- Write about one way that your life has become a combination of old and new.

- How do you get your daily news? Newspaper? TV? Internet? What do your favorite news sources say about you?

- Write about one popular new invention that you have emphatically rejected.

- Do you feel that twenty-four-hour TV cable news stations and internet news sites have helped or hurt the delivery of objective, serious news?

- Did anything else about this essay remind you of your own experiences? In your notebook, jot down one memory, thought or opinion that popped into your head as you were reading.

If You're Never Fully Dressed Without a Manicure, Then I've Been Naked All My Life

It was a week before the wedding and I was at the salon having my regular cut and color. My hairdresser and I were discussing the wedding day, what time she needed to come to my house, how many heads there would be to do, how much help she would need, what she would bring, when the make-up artist should come, how I should set up my dining room for them to work most efficiently, what styles the bride wanted etc., etc., etc. More details for an already long list.

Then she focused in on me. How was the dress coming? What kind of jewelry was I wearing? What color were my shoes? What did I want her to do with my hair? How were my nerves holding up?

So far so good. I had respectable answers for all of her questions except for the one that she had yet to ask.

"Where are you going to have your nails done?"

And there it was.

"I'm not."

"Wait. What? What are you saying?"

"I'm not going to have my nails done."

"But you're the mother of the bride!"

"Yes. I'm aware of that."

"BUT YOU'RE THE MOTHER OF THE BRIDE!"

"Well, yes, I know. But—"

"You cannot go to YOUR DAUGHTER'S WEDDING without a manicure."

"But my nails are awful. I never do anything with them beyond keeping them clean and clipping them short. A holdover from my younger days as a biter, I guess. I don't want to draw attention to them. Besides, I have too many other things to do. And besides that, I wouldn't even know where to go."

"You have to have your nails done."

"I don't want to."

"YOU HAVE TO HAVE YOUR NAILS DONE."

She was digging in. I was in a beauty salon. I had no allies here. I tried again.

"No one is going to look at my nails."

"EVERYONE is going to look at your nails."

"I don't notice people's nails, unless they're really long—like the kind that curl around themselves and tap on everything and make that hand useless—except for maybe holding a cigarette. Or waving goodbye—like the Queen!"

As I demonstrated, I smiled a little. A peace offering.

She didn't bite.

"You'll look unfinished. You might as well not do any of it if you're not going to do your nails."

She was angry with me. She has been doing my hair for years and years and we have talked about everything imaginable. But she never yelled at me before.

29

This was unsettling.

She finished covering my roots in goopy dye so my hair was sticking up in all directions and she had just swiped dye on my eyebrows. I was afraid she was going to walk away and leave me there looking like a cross between Medusa and Groucho Marx.

"Well, I know that the girls are going together to have a mani-pedi the day before. Maybe I'll tag along with them."

"Perfect. See to it that you do."

I wasn't sure that I would.

"And you're wearing open-toed shoes, so a pedicure is not optional."

Sigh.

*****

My mother had beautiful nails, hard and strong, nicely shaped and neatly painted. When she tapped them on a table, that table knew that it had been tapped. Even though she never had a professional manicure, her nails were always gorgeous and, if I misbehaved, potentially dangerous. One-poke wonders.

I didn't get the nail gene. I never developed the skill or the interest. Besides, biters like me have enough self-image issues without worrying about getting flecks of red nail polish on our teeth.

I had one previous manicure in my life—on my own wedding day. I stopped biting for three weeks prior in anticipation of that obligatory photo of the bride's hand over the groom's in front of the wedding cake, the one that shows off the new rings. It was a herculean effort and I was proud of myself for pulling it off, but I wasn't out of my wedding dress before I was picking at the nail polish and nibbling at my cuticles.

So I never understood the mani-pedi craze unfolding around me. It's an extravagance—a luxury that becomes a necessity when we forget how to live without it—like a microwave or a smart phone. It seems, though, that lots of people can't live without it. My town is filled with nail salons and mini-spas, and there's enough business to keep them going. I've discovered that some women I know go every couple of weeks with regular appointments scheduled months in advance. This was not a topic of conversation among my teacher friends, most too busy, too poor or too pragmatic to stress over their fingernails when there were so many other things to stress over—or pay for. So, in my defense, my nails have not been a source of embarrassment to me since I grew out of biting them.

Until now.

*****

When I arrived at the salon, the bridal party was already there. I was relieved that they were expecting me so I didn't have to tell anyone who I was or why I was there or what I wanted done. I was hoping that they would tell me.

I was ushered to an empty chair between my daughter and one of her bridesmaids. Good. They knew that I had no idea what to expect and would guide me discreetly through the process.

The place was brightly lit with manicure tables on one side of the room and pedicure chairs on the other. There were two big screen TVs on the wall above the manicure tables, one showing the news and one a Cameron Diaz film. Those perched in the pedicure chairs enjoyed optimum viewing. Both screens had the volume down and the closed-captioning activated. Soft music played and people spoke in hushed tones. I could hear the whirring of the massage chairs and the gentle sound of feet plopping in and out of foot baths behind me. I began to relax a little. I guess that's the point.

My manicurist was a young Asian girl whose English was fluent but heavily accented. She wore those invisible braces on her teeth and she spoke so quietly that I had to lean in to understand her.

"My nails are awful," I said. "I don't even know why I'm here."

"I make them beautiful," she said.

I believed her.

I told her that I wanted a French gel manicure. My daughter was having a French gel manicure and it was the only nail lingo I knew. She set to work and spoke very little after that. She filed and buffed and clipped and shaped with skill. She chose from an array of implements—emery boards of various thicknesses, clippers large and small, cuticle spoons and scissors, buffers that looked like the giant block erasers that accompanied those enormous, yellow elementary school pencils. I could see in her expression, focused and intent, that she was serious about the state of my fingernails. Her hands worked deftly, managing each tool with a dexterity that elevated the process in my estimation and made it suddenly meaningful.

A professional housepainter once told me that three quarters of his job was in the prep work. The actual painting, he said, was the least of it. If you skimped on the power washing and scraping and sanding and patching, it wouldn't matter how good a job you did painting. It would look like crap and last about twenty minutes.

I thought about that conversation now as I looked at my nails. Cuticles—pushed back. Hangnails—gone. Tips—curved. Surfaces—buffed. Shape—uniform and unlike anything I thought my raggedy nails could be.

Ms. Manicurist, I'm ready for my polish now.

But wait. First there must be the warm hand wax—four layers—followed by a warm-lotion massage from fingertips to elbows. I could feel the pre-wedding stress slip away and I was barely aware of what the girls around me were doing. I closed my eyes and I think I might have cried out a little when she put my palms together and wrapped the warm towels around my hands.

I'm sorry I doubted you. I didn't know. I just didn't know.

And now, at last, the polish.

As a teacher, I am a firm believer in professional distance, both figurative and literal. Never get too personal and never stand too close. But when you are a manicurist, you are not only no more than an arm's length away from your customer but you are also face-to-face at all times. Prying, paying eyes, watch every move you make, scrutinizing, judging, comparing. You are the victim of relentless observation. There's no room for mistakes. It must take nerves of steel.

From the beginning, I couldn't help but watch. My face was, after all, right there. And when the polishing commenced, I was fascinated by the dexterity and speed with which my manicurist applied several layers of variations-on-clear polish. She set a standard by which I will now judge all other manicurists. Before I knew it, she had applied all the base coats and was ready to paint on the white swish at the tips—the mark of the French manicure. Each one appeared in a single swipe and coordinated perfectly with the one that came before and the one that followed. Not a line out of place. Not a drop on my skin. And then, in a jiffy, a couple of clear coats on top. And through the whole process, her expression never changed. She never flinched. She hardly spoke. She just concentrated.

She is an artist. I understand that now.

*****

The pedicure was nice—the new technician, the massage chair, the leg massage, the warm, scented footbath, the nail shaping and polishing—but it didn't leave the same impression on me as the manicure did. Everyone in the room knew that this was my very first pedicure and they were amazed that I had waited this long to pamper myself. But I don't take well to pampering for its own sake and I felt sort of silly. After all, only two toes would show out of the openings in my wedding shoes. I could have easily taken care of those two toes myself with much less fuss. It's not that I feel that I didn't deserve to indulge a little, but I like my pampering to mean something. Toe nails don't require the same level of artistry that fingernails do. They are much easier to do on your own. Plus, you have to look down on the person doing it. And, you can't run away when it tickles.

*****

When all was said and done, I was astonished that people noticed my nails and commented on them, even after the wedding. And now that I have discovered the joy of the manicure, I look more at other women's nails—not just the wild ones, but the lovely, neat, well-attended ones as well. There is a pleasure in it that I had never considered, like appreciating an Italian boy's well-crafted haircut or admiring someone's funky, colorful, cleverly-tied scarf. It adds something to the beauty of the world and validates the artists in ways we like to see artists validated—with a living.

*****

My French gel manicure was gorgeous for two weeks. By the third week, it began to grow out and the temptation to pick at the polish curling up on my nail beds was irresistible. I tried but I soon realized that I wouldn't be able to remove the gel by myself.

So I had to go back to the salon. Tough break.

I had the gels removed and replaced with a regular polish this time. I decided to skip the pedi from now on and save the French gel for special occasions—like Christmas—so that it doesn't lose its appeal. I'd hate for the experience to become commonplace, but I look forward to doing it again.

In fact, I can't wait. And that's something I thought I'd never say.

Saving *Your* Life

- Write about your fingernails. What is your relationship with them? How do you care for them? What do they reveal about you?

- What aspects of your personal hygiene do you have done professionally? Which ones do you do yourself? Which ones do you ignore? Write about your experiences with haircuts, hairstyles, hair color, hair removal, make up, nails, tanning, wrinkle control, etc.

- What do you notice about other people's hygiene habits? Write about someone you've seen whose hair, nails or overall look attracts or repels you.

- What new thing have you tried lately that has surprised you?

- What have you avoided doing not because you didn't want to do it but because you were afraid you'd look stupid?

- Write about a time when you were shamed into doing something that you really didn't want to do. How did it go?

- What is your relationship with your hairdresser/barber? How does it compare to other friendships you have?

- How would you do in a job where your every move was scrutinized by your customer? Imagine a day in your current job when you were watched closely all day. How would you fare?

- Write about a job that you once underestimated, that you thought anyone could do. What happened to make you change your mind? How did you come to respect it?

- Did anything else about this essay remind you of your own experiences? In your notebook, jot down one memory, thought or opinion that popped into your head as you were reading.

MP3 Flashback

My MP3 player died.

Well, it's not actually dead yet. It turns on, the screen lights up and it lets me maneuver around. It seems to have most of what it came with—three games that I never played, categories for songs and videos and podcasts, a clock that runs only on standard time and a calendar that tells me that the date is December 23, 2005.

That is definitely not today.

While the factory default settings seem to be intact, everything that I downloaded into it over our years together is gone. When I try to sync it with my digital music account, I am told that my MP3 is in recovery mode and must be restored. This would seem encouraging, except that I have restored it several times now and at the completion of each restoration, my digital music account tells me that my MP3 is in recovery mode and must be restored.

So today I have it plugged into a resuscitator—er, my laptop—for one last try. I owe it that much before I bury it in a shoebox in the basement and start shopping for a new one. It is taking a charge, but it won't download the music from my digital music account that it puked out a month ago. In other words, it's still breathing, but it won't eat. It knows its name, but it can't remember mine.

I've lost hope.

And, as is so often the case, we don't realize how much something has meant to us until we are on the verge of losing it. So I started thinking about my MP3 journey, how long I lived quite happily without one and how it wheedled its way into my life and made itself utterly indispensable to me.

To that end, I unearthed the following essay, written by me on July 16, 2006. If we were making a movie, this would be the time that the picture would get blurry and the harp arpeggios would signal that we were about to embark on a journey to the past.

*****

An MP3 of One's Own

Virginia Woolf once said that a creative, independent woman needs some money and a room of her own. To that short list, I must add one more thing.

An MP3 digital music player.

I'm a high school teacher and the mother of two teenaged daughters. The MP3 craze began in my home on Christmas Day, 2004, when daughter number one was probably the last kid on her block to receive her very own juke-box-on-a-rope—a go everywhere, hide anywhere, five-thousand-song warehouse of sound. She thought it was about time. I thought we had just spent $300.00 to feed the beast that dwells deep within the Cabinet of Abandoned Electronics, the current home of an assortment of erstwhile cutting-edge gizmos that became obsolete before the wrapping paper hit the floor. Tickle its tummy, I thought, and it will spew out all sorts of portable music-making gadgets that would do the same job as this new kid. Better. Cheaper. Who really needs another one?

Well, after that Christmas, apparently all teenagers on earth.

My daughter hid her new earbuds under her long hair and could be tuned in always. In my classroom, I became an expert at ear-bud detection—under hair, under the hoods of sweatshirts, snaking up the backs of shirts. Even if the buds were well-concealed, I learned that a certain intensity of facial expression, which I originally mistook as interest in my lesson, actually revealed yet another carrier of contraband. I felt like I was fighting a cockroach infestation. As if holding kids' attention in school wasn't already hard enough.

And to think that I had contributed to the premature graying of other teachers by wiring my own kid.

As the 2005 school year wore on, I noticed MP3 players becoming less of a solitary pursuit and more of a social one. Unlike headphones which are easy to see and hard to share, earbuds are flexible and long enough for two heads at once. I'd see girls in homeroom, connected one head to the other by a thin white wire as they listened intently to a latest musical acquisition. A boy too afraid to ask a girl out could easily break the ice by offering an earbud to his dream date, plugging himself into the other one and enjoying three minutes of bliss (or torture) as he worked up the nerve to ask her to the movies on Saturday.

There was more to this than I realized. But I refused to see the truth. To me, these were just teeny CD players, enticing to kids because they could so easily drive the adults around them crazy. Let's face it; any kid would jump at the chance.

So, by Christmas of 2005, daughter number two was showing signs of MP3 readiness. Santa once again succumbed, but this time went with a junior-sized device with a smaller storage capacity. I rationalized that it could somehow do less damage, which just goes to show how even those of us on the front lines can deceive ourselves.

But something else was happening. By this time I had joined a gym. As I was puffing on the treadmill with my dinosaur headphones plugged into the six o'clock news, I noticed that the buff and beautiful around me wore armbands which I assumed at first were devices for measuring heart rate or blood pressure or ab ripples per second or the relative pressure of gluteal compressions per squeeze or something that could only matter to someone who looked hot in spandex. Then I saw them—the earbuds. MP3s! In the possession of *adults*! I was astounded. The invasion complete, I bought another one that Christmas, for my husband to take on his nightly walks.

From that point on, my home became digital music central. Everyone asked for digital music gift cards and among our email messages were digital music receipts and announcements of the free digital tune of the day. I remained stubbornly and perhaps naïvely loyal to the shoeboxes of CD's in the minivan until my family felt the need to drag me kicking and screaming into the twenty-first century. On Mother's Day, 2006, I was presented with my very own MP3 player. I oohed and aahed, thanked everyone for knowing just what I wanted, tossed the box into a drawer and paid it no mind until--last week.

And now, my life is forever changed.

My MP3 player, filled almost to capacity, is in the pocket of my jeans with the earbud wire snaked up under my shirt. One bud is in my left ear and the other dangles provocatively from the point of my V-neck T-shirt. I have taken to punctuating my conversations with the lyrics of whatever song has percolated to the top of the shuffle list. Sometimes I sing out randomly for the sheer joy of it. And sometimes the song in my left ear is my secret, and I get quiet and listen and maybe pop the right bud in for ultimate privacy. My song list is like a diary that I can choose to share or keep discreetly to myself. I can shift from Bocelli to Dylan, from *SPAMALOT* to *Wicked,* from The Beatles to The Soggy Bottom Boys, from Patsy Cline to Eva Cassidy, from Ray Charles to Mel Torme, from the Stones to Freddy and the Dreamers, or from *Manhattan* to *The Curse of the Black Pearl* at the smudge of a finger. My minivan is free of CD clutter for the first time ever. I feel free. I feel in control. I feel deliciously traitorous and just a little silly. I must admit that there is something to be said for having an MP3 of one's own.

*****

Do I hear a harp?

Things have changed since those days. I outgrew my little white MP3 and graduated to a sleek, silver, eighty-gig entertainment center that fit into the palm of my hand. There were earbuds, sure, but there was also a dock for communal listening at home and a system that plugged into the cigarette lighter for the car. My driving regimen—close door, buckle seatbelt, insert MP3 player into dock, sync station, click device on, check lipstick, adjust rearview mirror, hunt for sunglasses—was as automatic as breathing.

Interestingly, by the time I decided to go big or go home MP3-wise, my new friend already had the word *classic* in its name. I mean, the whole concept was just a few years old, but the devices changed and improved so fast that it was hard to keep track. Touchscreens, now *de rigueur*, were then squeezing out the click dial and the kids were already jumping ship. This made me hang on even tighter, although, to the hip-and-down-with-it, walking around with a Classic MP3 player is not all that different from pulling a portable cassette deck out of your fanny pack.

I didn't care. It worked for me. In fact, it worked very well, right up until it forgot who I was.

*****

The electronic device people have it all figured out. They have created things that change your life, that you can't live without and that you can't fix. The devices work for as long as they work and then they die. Period. We give them a proper burial and then go out and buy a new one. But chances are good that buying a new one does not mean buying another one like the one you had. The one you had might very well be obsolete, retired, relegated to the home. In fact, by then the whole concept might be outmoded. A device that just plays music and maybe lets you watch a movie? Really? Is that *all* it does?

One night I heard Jimmy Fallon say in his monologue that the company who made my MP3 player was going to stop manufacturing them all together. I had a hard time getting to sleep that night.

I have faced the fact that my well-worn Classic MP3 player is never coming back to me. I have not faced the fact that I may not be able to find another one, or, that if I do, it may be the last of its species that I'll ever see. I can't imagine anything that could replace it.

Wait! Why is everything blurry? And where *is* that harp music coming from?

*****

I run up the stairs to my bedroom. My bellbottom jeans, the hems wet and heavy from the rain, swish with every step. I make my way towards the small alcove, past the homemade macramé-and-driftwood wall hanging and through the strands of multi-colored hippie beads that hang at the portal. I lay down on the floor with my head positioned on a tie-dyed pillow placed between two small speakers and I smile up at the giant, orange Day-Glo peace sign painted on the ceiling. I reach over my head, grab a plastic box labeled *Mudslide Slim and the Blue Horizon* (James Taylor's newest), slip it in the slot of my brand-new eight-track tape player and press play. The tracks click and clunk into place and James sings "You've Got a Friend" to me as if he were in the room.

The sound is totally far out. What could *possibly* be better than this?

*****

What, indeed.

Saving *Your* Life

- How do you like your music delivered? Describe your relationship with your go-to gadgets.

- Trace the progression of musical appliances through your life. Try to remember your first of each device and how you used it.

- What is the oldest music delivery device that you remember? If it is a CD player, then we have nothing more to say to one another. If it is a record player for your 45s or a transistor radio, then we'll talk.

- What modern conveniences could you live without?

- What modern conveniences were you skeptical about when they first came out? How do you feel about them now? Why?

- Choose one device that you use now that did not exist when you were a kid. Describe what it does and how you completed that task without it once upon a time.

- We live in a time when our technology drives our lifestyle. Pick a device that has affected the way people behave and interact. How has it affected you?

- Close your eyes. Let the harps play. Flash back to an earlier time in your life when you thought things could never be better. Write about that time.

- Time will tell. What has it told you?

- Did anything else about this essay remind you of your own experiences? In your notebook, jot down one memory, thought or opinion that popped into your head as you were reading.

Fridge Detective

You can tell a lot about people by looking at their refrigerator doors.

When I go into someone's kitchen, my eye is immediately drawn to the magnets on the fridge and the stuff suspended beneath them. We all do it. It is, after all, public, right out there in plain sight, and though I feel that I'm being invited in by the kids' drawings and the vacation pictures and the funky magnets, I also feel like a busybody if I check it out too closely. Like I was peeking inside the family medicine cabinet or something. I'm always afraid that, stuck up there between Susie's drawing of a penguin and a post card from the orthodontist, I'll stumble across a reminder for Johnny's court date or an appointment card for a consultation with a sex therapist or a business card for a loan shark or a special VIP coupon for that restaurant that everyone knows is a front for a notorious crack dealer or some other embarrassing thing. I suppose it's not my fault if I discover a family secret or if I come to some disturbing conclusions from looking at the refrigerator door. I mean it's not like I'm snooping in the closets or anything. And while it's not exactly Facebook, we do put our *lives* up there, man, and anyone who comes into our homes can see—and judge.

But even if it doesn't give away deep, dark secrets, fridge stuff, like any choice we make in life, reveals something about the people who put it there. But what? That's where our powers of observation and deduction come in. People expose a little bit about themselves every time they open their mouths, pick a shirt, buy a book, open a door for someone else (or don't), drive too fast, walk too slow, choose a movie, pursue a profession, tip the waiter, forget to tie their shoes, doodle in a margin or take a picture. There is meaning in all of our actions should someone take the time to notice them. Writers, students of literature and detectives are always on the lookout for a trait revealed through actions and words. The rest of the world, perhaps, not so much.

We need to practice paying attention.

So I'm going to wriggle out on a limb here. I have a secret. Well, maybe not a secret so much as a quirk. (Right now my family is saying, "*A* quirk? Just one? Really?") Well maybe not a quirk so much as a hobby. It (among other things) is revealed in the potpourri of stuff on my refrigerator door. Put your deductive powers to work to see what you can tell about me from looking at my fridge. (You might be able to tell more by looking *in* my fridge, but I'm not offering that tour anytime soon.)

Here goes. Pay attention now. And take notes.

Stuck to our fridge, like fridges all over America, is a mish-mash of pictures, appointment reminders, invitations, business cards, coupons, decorative magnets, calendars and miscellany. Nieces and nephews smile out from under magnets that say things like, "Housework is Evil! It must be stopped!" and famous Mark Twain quotes, like, "In the first place, God made idiots. That was for practice. Then he made school boards." Among several clips and cats and cows, there's a magnet with a drawing of a nun with a wine glass labeled "Sister Mary Merlot," one of Teddy Roosevelt looking quite bully, one of an elderly Mark Twain posing in front of a window wearing a mortar board and academic robes over his white suit, one of a Renoir painting called "Monet Painting in his Garden in Argenteuil," which is actually a picture of a painting of Monet in his garden painting a picture of his garden, and one of the Beatles in their youth looking cocky and artsy and fabulous. Then there's one of the famous Cat in a Ruff (from a painting on the mantelpiece of the Mark Twain Hartford home), a pot-bellied panda bear, a Charlie Chaplin finger puppet, a 1" x 2" Cape Cod license plate, a Lake Placid landscape, a logo from The Today Show, a 2-D book that tells when the local library is open, souvenir magnets from Disney World, Hawthorne's House of Seven Gables in Salem and Jefferson's Monticello, three colorful, hand-made tin fish from Honduras and a bottle opener that is attached to a little Corona bottle containing a lime wedge floating in a suspicious yellow liquid.

What character assumptions can you make based on the aforementioned evidence? Of course, each of these items has its own little story, some worth telling, some not. Which ones would you ask me about if you could? Go back and review the list. Jot down your thoughts, Detective, and let's move on.

Under these magnets are the winning lotto tickets waiting to be cashed in for the windfall prize of $3.00, the volunteer usher schedule for a local theater company, the "Wish You Were Beer" postcard from our niece in Milwaukee, an invitation to a baby shower that I attended last weekend, a postcard from the Coliseum in Rome and another from a strip mine in Hibbing,

Minnesota, business cards from a DJ, a florist and a photographer and others from family entrepreneurs of whom we are proud, along with a 2016 calendar, a 2015 calendar, a 2014 calendar and the phone numbers of doctors, the dentist, the financial planner and our favorite take-out pizza house, the only one in town that offers a 100% whole-grain crust.

What have you added to your pool of evidence? What questions do you have? What assertions are you ready to make? Take a minute to collect your thoughts. When you are ready, go on.

Then there are, of course, pictures—school pictures, baby pictures, family pictures, a picture of my sister and her husband dancing at a wedding, a picture of me and Gene Wilder at a book signing, an I-won't-tell-you-how-old picture of my mom and dad and sister announcing the pregnancy that was to produce me, a picture of my kids with an avuncular Regis Philbin, a picture of my husband's mom doing one of her famous jigsaw puzzles, pictures of my children through the years in green shirts smiling from behind soccer balls, a picture of my very chilly kids with a distracted Matthew Broderick, the cousins at the lake, one of the daughters smiling alongside a very gracious Kiefer Sutherland, the cousins having a night on the town, a lovely family shot with Hank Azaria, a picture of a pleasant yet harried Jim Parsons signing my program, some passport mug shots, a dandy shot of me and the girls with David Hyde Pierce, another of our youngest at age two wearing Daddy's gigantic boots, another of me at a book signing across the table from a smiling Amy Tan, pictures of all of the beautiful great-nieces and nephews (which proves that our siblings are way older than us), a couple of me chatting with and getting a hug from Rob McClure, Tony-nominated star of the Broadway show *Chaplin* who will be a star someday, the cousins at Christmas, me with Livingston Taylor, me with John Sebastian, the most recent reminder card from the dentist, etc., etc., etc.

There are more, of course, but these are the highlights of the permanent collection. There is always the stuff that comes and goes—the occasional receipt, the unidentified phone number that never gets called, the recipe that I swear I'll try, a grocery list—but this is what you'd see there if you walked in today. What do you make of it? What questions would you like to ask? What catches your attention? What do you think is potentially revealing and what do you think has been revealed?

In literature as in life, we are at the mercy of our own powers of observation. Rarely is there an answer sheet to let us know if we are right or wrong. All we can do is add up the evidence and draw our conclusions based on what we have seen and heard. But first we have to notice stuff.

It's called critical thinking.

And the better we get at making observations and drawing conclusions from them, the more we become aware of what signals *we* are sending—by where we go and how we dress and what we read and what we write and, yes, what we display on our refrigerators.

With this in mind, I will leave you to your own devices to determine the secret, the quirk, the preference, the predilection of mine that is revealed on my refrigerator door.

The evidence is clear.

The conclusions are up to you.

Saving *Your* Life

- Look carefully at your fridge. What do you think it reveals about you and your family?

- What impression would you like people to have of you? Make a list of things that you could "plant" on your fridge that would suggest this to visitors.

- Create an imaginary fridge door for someone you don't like. What kinds of things might reveal his or her negative traits? (Caution: What might this exercise reveal about you?)

- Look around your home right now. If someone walked in unexpectedly, what would they discover about you?

- How is your home different when you are expecting company?

- How observant are you? Have you ever missed the signals even though they were there? Write about a time when you got it wrong even though the evidence was under your nose.

- Have you ever been misjudged? What signals did you send that were misinterpreted?

- Play Fridge Detective (or Car Detective or Classroom Detective or Desktop Detective or Kitchen Counter Detective or Bookshelf Detective or Coffee Table Detective or any other kind of detective you can think of that won't get you into trouble). Pay attention to the things that are there as well as the condition and arrangement of those things. The owners of these items are speaking to you. What are they saying?

- All good novelists let characters reveal themselves by what they say and do and how they interact with others. Pick a literary character you like and one that you don't like and think about what evidence the author presents that leads you to these conclusions.

- Did anything else about this essay remind you of your own experiences? In your notebook, jot down one memory, thought or opinion that popped into your head as you were reading.

Part Two
Mistakes Were Made

We do our best. We can't predict the future. Oh, sure, we can make educated guesses, but we can't know with absolute certainty that our actions are going to have the desired outcomes. Sometimes things go awry. Sometimes things backfire. Sometimes things explode.

If we worry too much about the forty-seven million ways life could go wrong, we'll freeze in our tracks. Uncertainty is life's one certainty. Moving forward means accepting the fact that things won't always happen the way we expect them to. We win when we try them anyway.

I'm not talking here about life's major moments, its glorious victories or crushing disappointments. Those events will get all the attention they deserve without my help. I'm talking about the little things—the getting-up-in-the-morning-and-making-your-way-through-the-day things that get tangled and snagged regardless of our best efforts. They're inevitable. And most of the time, they're pretty funny—at least in hindsight.

The following essays are chronicles of times like that.

What The Little One Saw

CAUTION: The following essay contains adult language, descriptions of violence and, worst of all, movie spoilers. Parental discretion is advised.

Pete, my friend and fellow blogger, writes eloquently about how movies and baseball helped to shape his decisions concerning the ethical upbringing of his son, fondly nicknamed The Knucklehead. A memorable post of his begins with a discussion of certain movies that make for edifying and satisfying family viewing, films that not only entertain, but also that kindle a love and knowledge of classic film. His methods obviously worked. His boy, now in college, has grown into an aficionado of cinema having been brought up on a diet of great films. He is also a really nice kid.

Pete is a good dad. He has carefully cultivated an educated film lover by introducing the right films at the right developmental moments. Check out his blog, *The Gentleman Knucklehead,* at www.dadofknucklehead.wordpress.com to see what I mean. Films like *A Hard Day's Night* and *A Night at the Opera,* as suggested in the post entitled "Walt Disney and The Knucklehead—Part One" are great choices for teaching kids about film technique and history when they think they're really just having a good time. It takes a thoughtful, committed parent to give his son such a gift.

I love classic films too, and I treated my kids to lots of them when they were growing up. Charlie Chaplin was a favorite. We enjoyed silent features like *The Kid* and *The Circus* and saw that there are many ways to communicate that don't include words. My older daughter was a very cute Halloween Chaplin in the third grade, complete with derby, cane, curly wig and moustache. True, most of her friends and even some of their parents had no idea who Chaplin was, and some may have questioned the wisdom of encouraging third-grade androgyny, but we got a kick out it. She looked cute and we took a lot of pictures. It didn't leave any noticeable scars.

But, unlike Pete, who seems to have had a plan in mind for his son's cinematic journey, our movie watching was much more haphazard—more of a working-mommy style education.

Our movie nights often went something like this.

"Here, kids. Pop this in the VCR while I make dinner, throw in a load of laundry, scrape the hours-old cat vomit off the carpet, vacuum up breakfast, chip the dried toothpaste off of the bathroom mirror and pull what we're all going to wear tomorrow out of the big pile on the living room floor. I *think* it's the clean pile. You settle in. I'll be right back."

I wasn't fooling anybody. If I got back at all, it was never *right* back. And then, the chances that I would sit down and stay awake for more than thirty seconds were slim to none. Their favorite movie-night joke was, "What movie should we pick for Mommy to sleep through tonight?" And then they'd laugh like it was the first time any of us had heard it. I slept through some of the finest movies ever made. These are the consequences of the teaching life and mornings that started before 5:30. At least the kids were watching good stuff. I hope. Regular TV was a crap shoot—then and now. I tried to provide quality fare and lead by example. Did it really matter if my eyes were closed?

So I guess it's not surprising that my kids seemed to get their most memorable movie lessons when I wasn't paying attention. And while the Knucklehead was served film that was age-appropriate and digestible, my youngest, in her most notable movie moments ever, got—the Coen Brothers.

Twice.

It's like the kid who goes around unnoticed by the adults at a party, sipping from unattended beer bottles. I still shudder.

*****

There are three things that you never want your seven-year-old to walk in on.

1) Daddy scarfing down the milk and cookies left on the hearth for Santa.

2) Mommy and Daddy having sex.

3) Any movie made by the Coen Brothers.

Now I have great respect for the films of the Coens. Joel and Ethan Coen have proved themselves to be the movie-making giants of their generation. They have been writing, directing and producing their own highly-regarded films for thirty years. These movies are thought-provoking, off-beat, dark, often violent and always well-crafted. They probe character in ways that rivet us to the screen while simultaneously making us squirm. Some of these films are horrifyingly funny while others are just funny and still others are just horrifying. As some of the finest and most memorable films of our age, they have been recognized by the industry's highest awards and rank among my all-time favorites.

But they are NOT kid-friendly.

So why did I let my seven-year-old and the Coen Brothers cross paths?

I will now testify on my own behalf.

*****

It has already been established that, after a long teaching day, watching a movie and remaining conscious was always a challenge for me. In my defense, I needed to watch the films in question at home because students brought them up in discussion in my high school film class and I, as any good teacher would, needed to brush up on the details. So, on fateful evening number one, in the best interests of my students and family alike, I left the children in Daddy's care, went up to my bedroom with the cassette of *Fargo,* closed the door and began my journey.

I was awakened who knows how much later by a knock on the door.

"Mommy, I can't sleep."

She came into the room. She stopped talking and stared, wide-eyed at the screen.

If you know this film, you know exactly what scene this was.

Still squinty, I looked at the TV and there it was--Steve Buscemi's foot sticking up out of the wood chipper, his blood spattered all over the pristine Minnesota snow.

I scrambled for the remote, but by the time I was awake enough to operate it, Frances MacDormand had already subdued Peter Stormare on the vast, frozen plain of this stark and unforgiving landscape.

In retrospect, I could have mitigated this horrific scene by just letting the video run a little longer. If she had seen MacDormand's gorgeous moments in the police car with her perp, where she recognizes the beauty in the bleakness around them and gives his evil a dose of her relentless Gunderson good, I might have had one less visitor in my bed that night.

We laugh about it now.

But wait! There's more.

On fateful evening number two, the scenario was similar. Kids with Dad. Mom upstairs. Planning for class. Not to be disturbed. Yadda, yadda, yadda.

The film this time? *The Big Lebowski.* As playful a romp as the Coens can muster. Certainly not something appropriate to use in a high school film class, at least not then, but my students were talking about it and I had never seen it through. If I was going to connect with them, I needed to be on top of what they were excited about. So, The Dude it was.

I learned a lot from my previous parental debacle. First, this time I would not lie down. Now this is not foolproof. I have been known to fall asleep sitting at the kitchen table with a fork in my hand. But sitting up while downing an atypical after-dinner cup of coffee should help. Next, I would set my alarm to go off every half hour.

Then, in order to have full access to the remote at a moment's notice, I simply would not put it down. And, since it is, for the most part, the language in this film and not the visuals that could prove disturbing to a child, all I had to do in the event of an intrusion was to press "Mute."

I had this.

Mom abides.

And, sure enough, the moment came when the door pushed opened and a little face popped in.

I immediately pressed "Mute." The TV obeyed. Success!

I relaxed and turned to the little girl in the doorway, a picture of innocence and sweetness. She was washed and jammied and her hair had been brushed and braided. Daddy had done a great job. She nodded affirmatively to my questions about snack and teeth and story and other bedtime rituals.

But she said nothing.

And she never took her eyes off the screen.

When it became clear to me that I was engaged in a monologue, I turned, for the first time since she entered the room, toward the TV.

John Goodman was driving along in a car with an unkempt Jeff Bridges in the passenger seat. Bridges was talking on the phone and seemed agitated. No big deal. The sound was muted. There was no violence, no wood chipper, no bloody foot, no scarlet snow. It was just two guys in a car.

And then I saw words on the bottom of the screen. I didn't take the time to read every one of them. I didn't have to. The important ones, the ones that jumped off the screen and took on a life on their own, created in my mind a sequence that looked something like this:

SHIT! FUCK! WHAT THE FUCK! SHIT! FUCK! FUCK YOU!
WE'RE FUCKED! FUCK, FUCK, FUCK, FUCK,
FUCKEDY FUCK!

I had somehow activated the Closed Captioning. And she, as we well knew, was a really, really good reader.

Are you fucking kidding me?

I felt guilty about this inappropriate foray into Coen-land for a long time. Nothing, she reminded me, that she didn't hear on the school bus. Small comfort there. Still and all, she came through it just fine. Now, many years later, she is a fan of good film and the Coens rank high on her list of favorites. Again, no visible scars.

Although, come to think of it, she does have a strange affinity for the color red—*and* a mouth like a truck driver.

Shit.

Saving *Your* Life

- Make a list of your ten all-time favorite films. What do you think this list says about you?

- Are any of your favorite films kid-appropriate? Which ones and why? And what about the others? Why not?

- Who directed the films on your top-ten list? If you don't know, find out at www.IMDB.com. While you're there, see what else these directors have done.

- Pick a film from your list and convince a parent to allow/not allow his kids to watch it.

- Pick a film that you'd like to share with your child. Jot down questions that you might ask before, during and after viewing to spark discussion and reinforce understanding.

- Have you ever compared your parenting with the methods of someone else? (Who hasn't?) Whose methods would you emulate and why?

- Who is the worst parent you know? Why do you think so? How are you different?

- What moments of adulthood did you glimpse as a child? What effect did this have on you? Were you different afterwards?

- What mistakes have you made around kids that you still regret? What mistakes have you made that you can now laugh about?

- How many Coen Brothers films can you name? Check yourself at www.IMDB.com. How many have you seen? Review your favorites. Bash your least favorites.

- Did anything else about this essay remind you of your own experiences? In your notebook, jot down one memory, thought or opinion that popped into your head as you were reading.

GOT 'EM!

My heart is pounding and I feel as if I have just run a mile without ever having left my kitchen table. I feel exhilarated, exhausted and more than a little angry. But I got 'em. I got 'em, all right. It was twenty-three minutes of terrifying, white-knuckle suspense, but I won. I got 'em. They're mine.

Excuse me for a moment while I catch my breath.

Whew!

There are many reasons for purposely putting ourselves through an ordeal. There are many ways we can pit ourselves against the odds to prove our mettle to the world. There are many paths we can take to show what we're made of, to display our determination, our doggedness, our true grit.

One of these, for me, is buying concert tickets.

It was promotional genius to put Bruno Mars concert tickets on sale the morning after his performance at Super Bowl XLVIII. He is one of those rare performers whose style appeals to kids and boomers. The kids love that he sings about sex and that his show is loud and boisterous and rebellious. Boomers see in him a rebirth of all of their favorite Motown acts and how they used to move and groove back in the day. Mars' footwork conjures up memories of James Brown and his pipes wrap together the best of Michael, Smokey, Tops, Temptations and fill-in-your-fave-here. Flashy jackets and ties add a touch of in-your-face class and it doesn't hurt that Bruno is a real cutie patootie from any angle. Watching him is fun. It gets my motor running. It makes me feel young.

I want me some more of that.

So we checked out his summer tour schedule and, lo and behold, his website said he would be appearing in a concert venue near me and tickets would go on sale on Monday morning, 10 a.m.

What luck!

At 9:45 a.m. I set myself up at the kitchen table with my computer and a second cup of coffee and prepared to make quick work of adding Bruno to our summer concert schedule. My husband, who usually does the ticket buying, cautioned me that I could be in for a frustrating time of it, but I pooh-poohed his warning, attributing it to his detail-obsessed dominant left brain. It'd be fine. Quick. Painless. Click. Done.

By 9:55 I was on the ticket site, calm, poised, confident, ready. Working the Monday morning crossword puzzle to pass the time. In ink. Sipping the coffee. Everything under control.

Then, at the stroke of 10, the page came up, the game clock flashed in my face, the bottom fell out of my poise and the race was on.

I tried to be responsible and read my options before committing to anything, but I knew that online tickets sell out in seconds and I was feeling the pressure. I chose my *Quantity*— Two. Easy. *Ticket Type*—Full Price. No real choice to be made here, unfortunately. Also easy. *Price and Section*—$149.50 for the front section? That's too expensive. Way too expensive.

$46.00 for the lawn? I'm too old for the lawn. Way too old. What's left? Rear pavilion. $55.50. A bargain. Click *Find Tickets*. Type in the security phrase. Click *Continue*.

Relax as the dots go around and around and the page tells me I have fewer than three minutes to wait. Way fewer as it turned out. I looked out the window to see a squirrel wedge his entire body into the bird feeder and when I looked back I had two seat numbers staring at me and one minute and twenty-one seconds to decide if I wanted them. Twenty. Nineteen. Eighteen. Seventeen. Sixteen...

"Of course I want, them, you idiot!"

The screen is, of course, not voice activated.

I found the place, rose from my seat and, with seventeen seconds to spare, feverishly clicked *Buy Tickets*.

YEAH! What a rush!

I fell back into my chair. I was home free. The next page came up asking me how I wanted my tickets delivered. MY tickets! Success is sweet! I clicked *Print From Home*.

It was 10:05.

It was like that moment in *Apollo 13* when Kevin Bacon clicks the toggle that mixes the fuel that later blows out the engines and sends them all hurtling uncontrollably through space.

The circle of dots on the page that said *Processing Your Request* circled. And circled. And circled.

And stopped.

I can't remember exactly what it said next. My eyes were blurred with tears. But it was something like "We're Sorry. We just wasted what must feel like hours of your life. We can't do the very simple thing you asked us to do, even though you were willing to pay for the privilege, and we led you to believe that all was well and that you and your daughter were on your way to enjoying a youthful, life-affirming evening of fun and music at our venue. We screwed up. Please return to the previous page."

Every page to this point warned me vigorously that I could NOT return to a previous page without falling out of the queue.

I had nowhere else to go.

I returned to the previous page.

I fell out of the queue.

It was 10:08.

I was right back where I started from. Only this time, my coffee was cold, my unfinished crossword was on the floor and my confidence was shaken. I felt betrayed. Why does it have to be this way? Why? While this was certainly easier than standing in line at the box office for hours, it was much harder for me to understand how I could be a failure at *clicking*. People *get* tickets. People *I know* get tickets. *My husband* gets tickets. It shouldn't be this hard! I was sure, though, that I missed my chance, that the show would be sold out, that I should just give up on this sorry attempt at finding the fountain of youth, that I should do something adult with my life, that I should leave the ticket-getting to the nimble and move on.

So, of course, I had no choice but to try again.

This time, I had experience on my side. I knew what I wanted and what to expect. But the ticking clock at every step of the process created a sense of urgency that was disarming. As it turned out, there was plenty of time to complete each task, but it felt like there was a proctor standing up in front of the room with a stopwatch. It activates the body's fight or flight reflex.

Adrenaline flows. Heart rate increases. Muscles stiffen.

I click with feigned authority. Two. Full Price. Rear Pavilion. *Find Tickets.*

All right. They're searching. Only this time the search started out at fifteen minutes instead of three. And that number flitted about with abandon, paying no regard to sequence or the laws of physics. Fifteen slipped to eleven and back to fourteen before plummeting to one and then back up to ten. It was maddening. Unable to just sit and stare at the screen, I reached for a pillow that I was crocheting to at least keep my hands busy. I looked outside and saw that the damned squirrel was still in the feeder and had just about emptied it. I don't know why the birds don't flock up on him and peck him to death. There are enough of them. I try to control nature, but, really, I can't be everywhere. I yelled from my place at the table to no avail. I knew that if I moved I would once again jeopardize my tickets and everything they had come to represent. So I stayed put, trying to relive my youth while crocheting a pillow and talking to squirrels.

The screen flashed. I dropped my hook.

I have seats! They are a few rows *behind* the first ones and $10.00 *more* expensive. What? Don't ask questions! Take them. TAKE THEM! The dots are circling. THE DOTS ARE CIRCLING!

Click. *Buy Tickets.*

How would you like them delivered?

Oh, God.

Had the system been working on Apollo 13, Kevin Bacon's toggle click would have been just another necessary step in the process. There was no other way to do what had to be done. If he had another try, he would, out of necessity, have done exactly the same thing.

Click. *Print From Home.*

It was 10:17.

Certainty of failure sweetens the joy of success. After just a couple of dot rotations, up popped the payment screen. If this were a movie, we would slip into slow motion as I tip back my chair, leap to my feet, pump my fists in the air and shake the rafters with an ecstatic YES! YES!! YES!!! Normal speed would resume as I come back to my senses long enough to make sure that I complete the transaction and check the time.

10:23.

You know the rest.

And now, as I recover from twenty-three minutes of hell, it occurs to me that Dave Matthews tickets go on sale next week.

Bring it on.

Saving *Your* Life

- What do you do to keep yourself in the game? What keeps you moving, active and youthful?

- What is your relationship with birds and squirrels?

- What was your last struggle with technology? Who won?

- List activities that you once did differently than you do now—like buying concert tickets. Shoot for ten.

- Pick one item from the above list and compare the old to the new. Is it really an improvement?

- "Certainty of failure sweetens the joy of success." List examples of when this has been true for you. Or do you disagree?

- Does Bruno Mars' music and showmanship appeal to you? Who would you pay money to see?

- Write about some of your favorite concert memories.

- Write about something you did that you thought would be easy—but wasn't.

- Did anything else about this essay remind you of your own experiences? In your notebook, jot down one memory, thought or opinion that popped into your head as you were reading.

The Wine Shrine

Gift-buying is so much easier when the people we buy for are obsessed with something. People addicted to hobbies—like books or sports or collections or travel or crafts—are always in need of something new to support their passions and are always flattered when we remember what they like. So when we buy a book by some obscure writer or hard-to-get tickets to a game or a colorful elephant figurine (trunk up, of course) or some new hi-tech way of keeping a passport safe or the latest in skiwear and we match these things up with the right people—fireworks happen. Joy abounds, we look good and all is right with the world.

Let's eat cake.

But it's almost never that easy. Or that affordable. Or that successful. Sometimes—most of the time—we don't know what people have, what they like or what they want. If they are teenagers, or in-laws, we're probably dead in the water before we ever even hit the mall.

We all have evidence of the gift-giving mistakes we've made, the money we've wasted and the good will we've squandered. All we have to do is look around the house to find last year's CDs and DVDs still shrink-wrapped, the wrong team's hoodie in a heap in the corner with the tags still attached, unread books, uneaten treats, games played once, that green sweater in our daughter's closet that we could have sworn that we bought in blue or that frilly birthday blouse that auntie gave us—the one that *we* gave *her* last year. Each gift was the perfect thing at the time. Yep. Nailed it.

Or not.

So, it's time to take a new approach. We have to take charge of this gift-giving thing and make it work to our own advantage. We need to find a never-fail, sure-fire, bulls-eye-every-time method that will make them happy, make us look good and make shopping a breeze. This may sound too good to be true, but I think that I have found a way.

All we have to do is to be the one to start everyone off on a new obsession.

*****

Remember Add-a-Pearl necklaces? According to their website, they've been around since 1854. Zillions of grandmas started zillions of little girls on these necklaces for over a hundred and sixty years. And once you start one of these, you have no choice but to continue the tradition. Nothing is sadder that an Add-a-Pearl to which no pearls have been added. So you have to commit. But once you do, this gift is yours to give. You have dibs for as long as it takes. When the necklace is done, in, say, twenty years, it is a gift from Grandma and only Grandma. And for twenty years, Grandma didn't have to wrack her brains over what to get that kid who has everything. Whatever else she may have bought that the kid loved or hated, the pearl was always there for that ceremonial birthday-party moment when the sugared-up wild child knew she'd better stop flying around the room like a hornet and sit quietly on Grandma's lap for the thirty seconds that it took to slip the new pearl on the chain. And even if the kid writhed and squirmed, together they created the one gift that would eventually mean something and be remembered. Something that would be there forever. A tradition. An heirloom.

Did that kid ever ask for an Add-a-Pearl necklace? No. Did she even know that they existed? No. Did she look forward to that Grandma Moment every birthday? Maybe secretly. Does she treasure that necklace? Now she does, yes. She wore it on her wedding day.

Get the picture?

*****

When I was a kid, grocery stores had these serial promotions. (There were *cereal* promotions as well, but that's another subject.) A new item in the set—glassware, dishes, pots and pans—would be introduced each week. The first week, the thing was dirt cheap and after that the price went up to where it would stay for the duration of the promotion. My mother often bought the first installment of whatever it was and then she'd somehow resist the rest. Sometimes the promotion would be kids' encyclopedias—hard cover, illustrated in full color, easy to read. Mom was pretty tight with the grocery money, but since the introductory price was only forty-nine cents, she'd buy me the first volume. But the next week, when the price went up to $1.99, she threw on the brakes. When I fussed about how much I loved the first book, she'd buy the B volume to shut me up and then she'd stop taking me shopping with her until the promotion was over.

I wanted the rest of every set so much. But Mom never gave in. By the time I got older and the store stopped this sort of thing, I had the A and B volumes of at least three different sets of encyclopedias and I knew everything there was to know about aardvarks, asteroids, amoebae, Beethoven and badgers. But if Mom had played her cards right, she could have bought up the volumes and meted them out as gifts for a year—C-D for Valentine's Day, E-F-G in my Easter basket, H-I-J-K on rainy days during summer vacation, L-M-N-O-P for my birthday and the motherlode of Q-R-S-T-U-V-W-X-Y-Z under the Christmas tree.

The point is that once you have the first installment of something, the rest of the collection begs to follow. And it's even better if someone else will buy them for you, whether you knew that you wanted them or not.

For grandmas and other gift-givers, this is important information to remember.

If you're in it for the gift-giving long haul with someone, all you have to do is to start him or her off with Volume One of anything and the love will follow.

Retail America is totally in our corner on this one. Everything comes in sets and series and collections and assortments. And once you love one of something, doesn't it stand to reason that you'll love two?

Or twelve?

*****

We are buying presents all the time in my family and sometimes shopping for them can be a real pain in the ass. But once you get your family members started on their own little collectible journeys, it gets easier. There's always at least one gift that you know they'll like because they already told you so—or you told them. Here's some of the merch that has worked for me.

Charm bracelets are great for all ages, and, if you pick the right company, there are charms for kids and for adults and for collectors and for casual wear and for dress. All interests. All prices. All of the women and girls in my family have bracelets and a new charm is a can't-miss gift.

I recently started a young niece on a collection of those single-charm bangle bracelets with endless charm designs. They look best on the arm in multiples and are worn by women and girls and even teenagers (imagine that!), so now I will be in charge of adding to her collection for the rest of my life.

Collectible figurines (a new one for every important occasion), snow globes, music boxes—all have found their way into my curio cabinet over the years. Some were gifts to me, but most were gifts from me to my daughters who, someday, will take them and decorate their own homes with them. I hope.

Independent authors are encouraged to write books in series for good reason. People who like the first one will keep buying them. If you can interest someone in a book series or in the works of a particular (hopefully prolific) author, then you've got birthdays covered for as long as those books keep on coming. There are seven *Harry Potter* books and no one can read just one. When I was a kid, an *Archie* comic book or a new *Nancy Drew* brought me pleasure times two. First, I got to read it and second,

I got to add it to the shelf and admire the collection. Double whammy.

Dolls, action figures, little metal things on wheels, building sets, stuffed critters—toy stores are full of collections that kids don't even know they want. All you have to do is to be the one who gives that kid the first Matchbox car or Barbie or Beanie Baby or set of Legos and you are in for a good long run.

With kids, you need to get them hooked early and you need to be the first to do it. The fast food industry and toy manufacturers have known this for years.

*****

Making this work for adults may require more stealth. Starting a new collection for an older person is tricky. Unless this is someone you live with, you never know what might already be lurking in the basement. So what you need to do here is to listen very carefully for any hint of a crush—a team, an actor, a singer, an activity, a vacation spot, a flower, a bird, a mode of transportation, a craft, a drink, an artist, a composer, a TV show, an exercise regimen, a food, a body of water, a fish, etc., etc., etc. This must be a very deliberate on your part and you must be ready to slip into the bathroom at any moment to write down your findings.

Then, jump on it. What you will create here is not so much a collection, but a brand. And once you create it, the secret's out. Unlike the exclusivity of the Add-a-Pearl arrangement, a brand is a wide-open thing. Others will weasel in on it before you can get to the next occasion. Shopping must commence at once.

My husband is a Dolphins fan. This is a source of amusement

for me—both because of the team's record and because of its teal and orange team colors. But when he is out shoveling the driveway in a blizzard wearing his Dolphin gear—hat, jacket, gloves, scarf—we never have to worry about losing him in the snow. He can curl up afterwards in his teal and orange Snuggie, rest his head on his teal and orange team pillow and sip hot chocolate from a teal and orange team mug that practically glows in the dark. Teal and orange socks, ties, Christmas ornaments, bobble heads, t-shirts, sweatshirts, fridge magnets, license plate holders—over the years he has unwrapped them all, some from me, some from the girls, and some from extended family and co-workers who busted in on the brand. The franchise may not win games, but it produces enough stuff to make him smile on every gift-giving occasion and to clutter my house forever.

My mother once let it slip that she liked owls. Sadly, I was not the only one to pick up on this pronouncement, and, as my mother was notoriously difficult to buy for, the owl branding began in earnest from several family camps. We discovered that there was almost as much owl stuff out there as there was Dolphin stuff. But I struck gold when I found a collection of decorative owl plates, signed, framed and suitable for hanging. Lovely—and expensive. I bought them all and it took eight gift-giving occasions to complete the set. We did the same for my mother-in-law, who had a love of songbirds. They both displayed the plates for many years and seemed to like them. When both moms passed, all sixteen plates returned to me.

I hadn't counted on that at all.

My younger daughter has very sensitive skin and she loves things that are soft and snuggly. I was not able to keep that a secret for very long and now she has more fleece blankets, fluffy towels, flannel sheets and fuzzy slippers than one girl could ever use. There are not enough closets in my house to store them.

My older daughter, always a tough one to pin down gift-wise, loves games—board games, card games, puzzles. She has been collecting them for a while now, thanks to birthdays and Christmas, so, as the family cruise director, she would be in charge of what we played on game nights. It was fun. But, when she married and moved to a small apartment in another state, she left the games, and all of her other collectibles, here.

*****

Hmm. Well, now that I think about it, this plan has its disadvantages. Once you create a brand for someone, you do run the risk of it becoming more *your* obsession than theirs, especially when you think you've solved the problem of the hard-to-buy-for. My mother once let it slip that while she liked owls, she didn't *like them* like them and the proliferation of them in her house freaked her out sometimes—especially late at night. And, while my husband remains a die-hard Dolphins fan, he is not a fan of dressing in teal and orange and prefers to fly a tad more under the fashion radar. The Beanie Babies, though much-loved, overran the girls' bedrooms, as did the American Girl dolls, the Dear America books and the fully-accessorized critters from Build-a-Bear. It seems that when gifts are easier to find, everybody wants to get in on the act. And then, before you know it, the closets overflow, the curio cabinets bulge, the book shelves heave, the doors don't close and you wonder how this happened.

And, just when you think your kids don't pay attention to a

fraction of what you are trying to teach them, it turns out that they've been watching you a lot closer than you knew.

I always thought that I was an open book as far as gift options were concerned. I'm pretty clear on the music I like to listen to, the books I want to read, the jewelry I wear. Clothes are an issue, I know, because I'm never the same size for two gift-giving occasions in a row, but I always shop in the same stores, so gift cards should be a snap. I love scarves and will wear a new one whether or not it matches anything I own. I always need crochet supplies, guitar picks, ukulele music (or maybe lessons) and you can never go wrong with a day at a museum, a trip to a restaurant or tickets to a movie.

I didn't think I was difficult to buy for until it became clear to me that my family thought I was. How did I discover it?

Well, it seems that even I have been branded.

*****

I never saw it coming. Even when it was happening, I didn't catch on. Then, one day, it hit me.

If recently received gifts are any indication, and I truly believe they are, then my family thinks I'm a wino.

Now, I enjoy a nice glass of wine with dinner. Maybe two. But I never thought of it as a way of defining myself.

True, wine-drinking women are quite fashionable these days. TV is especially aware of this and we can watch many of its women, among them Frankie and Grace, Hoda and Kathi Lee, Penny and Bernadette and even Amy Farrah Fowler, tipping back the stemware. Wine has become the smart woman's refreshment of choice and there is plenty of room on the bandwagon for all. Merchants discovered this niche market and have exploded it, creating innumerable products that both create and perpetuate the stereotype of the smart, classy, hard-working, wine-swilling, modern American woman. The wine, it seems, is the least of it.

And now, slowly, stealthily, almost imperceptibly, these items have gifted their way into my home.

See for yourself.

First, there are plaques. The one that sits on the ledge of my stove has a quote attributed to W.C Fields which says, "I cook with wine. Sometimes I even use it in the food." For some reason, visitors to my home seem to like that one. Another says, "A Meal Without Wine is Called Breakfast." This is not a routine I advocate, unless I am traveling in Italy where it becomes oddly acceptable—and accurate. And no kitchen is complete without a plaque that says "Coffee Keeps You Busy Until It's Time To Drink Wine."

Then there are the cocktail napkins with witty sayings like, "Wine a Little—You'll Feel Better" and "Well Red." That design, with a full wine glass poised over an open book, also appears in my closet as a tee-shirt with shiny red sequins filling the glass. So chic.

Christmas brings out the wine glass stem charms—the balls of different colors and the little toys that light up and flash. The technology is amazing when you think about it. And where would I be without my decorative wine bottle stoppers? There's the one with the big red Christmas ball, another with a lovely snowflake and a third that boldly chants, "Merlot!" These, along with pretty wine bottle bags and cute little Santa bottle outfits make for fun party conversation and I am careful to pack them neatly away after the holidays so that they will be safe and secure until their next annual appearance.

Corks are ubiquitous in wine circles and one must have an attractive receptacle for them. My daughter gave me an oversized wire wine bottle to hold mine. I was amazed, frankly, at how fast I filled it up and needed more space. So my niece bought me a kit that uses stick-pins to turn corks into cute little people. And, of course, a cork still in a bottle must find its way out, so a friend gave me an electronic cork-taker-outer—faster, easier and a lot more fun than *any* manual version. It sits in its charger on my counter so it's always at the ready.

Temperature? Well, reds are not a problem. But summer whites take up fridge space, so my youngest bought me a dedicated, temperature-controlled chest that holds six bottles at a time and another niece added an electronic ice bucket that chills two more. So that gives me the potential of having eight crisp, perfectly chilled whites ready to go at any given time. Party's apparently at my house.

And, of course, nothing says Mom like the giant wine glass that says, "Mom's Wine Glass," or the dangly grape cluster charm bangle bracelet, or the "Sister Mary Merlot" refrigerator magnet which conveniently embraces two obsessions, wine and nuns, in one clever gift. The Tuscan wine and cheese table painted in rustic tones on the giant magnet that covers the face of my dishwasher makes a bold statement in my kitchen. That properly chilled bottle of prosecco will generate warm toasts to the givers some summer afternoon and I will enjoy the gift cards for winery tours and tastings come spring.

So, it seems that over the years the branding process has made my home a shrine to wine. I'm not sure whether I started it or it was started for me, but it has taken on a life, even a culture, of its own, far beyond that of owls and song birds and Dolphin Wear and Add-a-Pearls.

I'm not sure how I feel about this.

Let's discuss it over a nice Italian red, shall we? Sangiovese, maybe?

Salute!

Saving *Your* Life

- Have you been branded? If so, then this is a way that some people define you. Are you good with it?

- Have you ever purposely branded someone to make gift-giving easier for you? How did it go? Any repercussions?

- What do you wish people would buy for you? How might you get the word out?

- How do you feel about gift-giving in general? Is it frustrating, satisfying, stressful, joyful?

- If you could do away with gift-giving in your life, would you? Would you replace it with some other sign of affection or just let it go?

- Who is the most difficult person in your life to buy gifts for? Why? Describe some gifts you struggled over.

- Who is the easiest person in your life to buy gifts for? Why? Describe some of your gift successes.

- Describe a gift disaster that you were a part of.

- Have you ever bought people gifts they didn't want because you thought they should have them?

- What do you do with gifts that you don't like?

- What do you have too much of in your house? How do you stay on top of it? Or do you?

- Were your children over-gifted? What became of the stuff as they grew out of it?

- Were you surprised by the gifts your kids loved and the gifts they ignored?

- Who gets you the perfect gift every time? Anyone? What are some examples?

- Have you ever found yourself sucked into the very latest gifting trend? What was it, who was it for and how did you fare?

- How long have you stuck with a series of gifts for someone? Ever drop the ball? Has anyone ever stopped buying you gifts in a series that you were enjoying?

- Did anything else about this essay remind you of your own experiences? In your notebook, jot down one memory, thought or opinion that popped into your head as you were reading.

Part Three
Woodpecker Wars

Humans believe that we have an answer for pretty much everything. We beat the odds by treating and curing diseases. We shrink distance by building contraptions that get us places fast. We defy gravity by flying around our world and beyond. We master land, sea and sky by predicting earthquakes, tornadoes, volcanic eruptions, tsunamis, summer showers, salmon migrations and solar eclipses. We believe that we are large and in charge and that we are entitled to our smugness. There is nothing we can't learn to control.

This attitude is ingrained in us—no mountain too high, no ocean too wide, no bird too obnoxious. Fortitude is what it takes. Grit. Determination. Brains. Courage. These things all come standard on our model. We've got this—whatever it is.

But then, one day, out of nowhere, comes a cute little red-capped bird that challenges our authority and shakes our confidence to its very core.

And then the lines are drawn. The die is cast. The gauntlet is thrown. The war is on and our mettle is tested.

Who will win? There was a time when I wouldn't even have thought to ask the question. Now I must.

The battle has been fierce, the encounter protracted. Victory is no longer assumed.

I fear the worst.

Woodpecker Wars
Episode One
He Is Not Afraid Of Me

We like birds. We are not bird-watchers by avocation, but we like having them around. We have a lot of trees in the back yard and it's fun in the summer to sit out there, listen to the different songs and watch the activity in the tree tops. Some days the swooping and diving and screeching and dog-fighting is like watching the avian version of *Wings, Captain Eddie* and *Snoopy vs. The Red Baron* all rolled into one. Other days, as we are among the few homeowners in our neighborhood who don't apply chemical treatments to our lawn, birds of assorted species gather in peace to peck for worms, grubs, insects and dandelion seeds and to fatten themselves up for whatever seasonal life-altering event is forthcoming. The sugar feeder, after weeks and weeks of attracting nothing but bees and ants, has finally caught the attention of hummingbirds. And in the winter, we will fill a large wooden feeder with seeds and let the feathery die-hards duke it out with the squirrels.

All in all, we are good to them. We give them tall trees and bugs and seeds and validation. We give them a haven from roaming cats and little boys with BB guns. We give them attention and, occasionally, applause. Most are appreciative. One, a cowbird we think, has even been bold enough to consider herself a friend. She sits on the back of a patio chair to chat with us and follows my husband around when he mows the lawn.

For the most part we have been rewarded with a yard full of color and drama and song. Cardinals, blue jays, purple finches, gold finches, hawks, mockingbirds, blackbirds, chickadees, mourning doves, tufted titmice, orioles, cedar waxwings, geese, ducks, robins, crows, grackles, starlings, juncos, sparrows and even great blue herons have visited our yard at one time or another. Those that are brave enough to face a New England winter are regulars at our feeder and the others are a welcome sight in the spring.

Except for one.

*****

It started in April. I was awakened one morning not by the sweet song of birdies in the treetops, but by machine gun fire on the metal rim of my bedroom skylight. The next day, it was the rain gutter. The day after that, it was both, first one and then the other. What the hell?

A woodpecker, that's what.

Now, we have entertained woodpeckers regularly and have welcomed them. It *was* (and I emphasize the past tense) fun to watch them peck away at the bark looking for whatever it is that they look for. We have seen an assortment of types, but, as it turns out, the smallest and cutest of them is also the boldest and most infuriating. When the adorable little Downy decided that my house was preferable to the trees as a pecking place, our friendship ended.

And the war began. A war, by the way, that I am losing.

The Downy Woodpecker is about six inches tall. If you stretch your thumb and middle finger as far apart as you can and measure from tip to tip, you have an idea of how small this maddening little pecker-head really is. Ours is a male, white-bellied with black and white speckly wings, a black and white striped head and a little red cap, reminiscent of the fight-to-the-death revolutionaries in Dickens' *A Tale of Two Cities*. He is cute, but as we discovered, his petite stature belies his hubris. Apparently, in the woodpecker world, size doesn't matter.

The rapid-fire rat-a-tat subsided as the weather got warmer and I thought that the problem had solved itself. I forgot about it and went about my life, had a busy summer planning my daughter's wedding, basked in the afterglow of a very beautiful event, had a restful, early-September, post-wedding recuperation vacation on Cape Cod and returned home to find several holes pecked into the side of my house.

I found them one morning when I was writing at the table on my porch. The porch is a former deck off the back of my house that has been roofed and screened in. It has a southern exposure and so, when the screens are replaced by windows, it stays warm enough to use on sunny days well into the fall. It is my favorite place to write. With a sweatshirt, fuzzy slippers, a cup of coffee and sometimes an afghan, I try to stretch out porch season as long as I can. I dread the day when the inevitable cold blasts of winter will force me inside until spring.

Anyway, one morning shortly after my return from the Cape, I settled in on the porch with my breakfast and my laptop. I wasn't a paragraph into a new essay before I heard it—rat-a-tat, rat-a-tat, r-r-rat-t-t-at-t-tat-t-t. Not on metal this time, but wood. I enjoyed it, thinking it was the sound of a woodpecker in a tree. But then, as the pecking persisted, it occurred to me that it was too close, too solid sounding, too menacing to be a bird in a tree. My investigation took me out the door, to my right and around to the side of the house. There he was, the little culprit, clinging to the molding, pecking away at my house as if it were his to peck. I yelled and clapped my hands and successfully chased him into a nearby tree where he perched himself and waited for me to go back inside so that he could resume demolition. I did. Then he did. I went back out and chased him again. He made it clear to me even then that I am little more than an annoyance to him, a nuisance, an interruption. I do not pose a threat. Not even a little one. Not even when I throw rocks.

He comes every day. So now every day I go out to chase him. I keep rocks ready in a little bowl on my writing table on the porch so that I don't have to waste time searching the ground for them. I never attempt to hit him with the rocks. I couldn't if I wanted to. They are just to make noise when I bounce them off of the house or hurl them into the small, nearby fir tree where he sits to wait out my tirade. My presence alone, enough to chase most any other bird, is not sufficient for this little tyrant. I could stand under him all day and he would continue to peck unfazed. He moves only when I make a fool of myself and even then it's temporary. My most fearsome assaults are, to him, a source of amusement.

He is not afraid of me.

The hole count continues to rise. We are up to six with no end in sight. In fact, he is moving from the corner molding to the shingles themselves. Since yelling and flailing and flinging rocks wildly at my own house have proven ineffective deterrents, I am, at this moment, losing the battle. But this is only a temporary setback because I have something that my pea-brained adversary doesn't have.

Internet access!

I will find a Plan B. There is a war to win and I have not yet begun to fight!

*****

Picoides pubescens.

This is the Downy Woodpecker's scientific name and it is the first thing I learn when I Google him. It tells me a lot. According to Bing, in zoology, "pubescens" means "covered with down or fine short hair"—hence the "downy"—but, after thirty-six years teaching high school, to me, "pubescens" sounds a lot like "adolescence" which loosely translates into the mantra, "All attitude all the time." Suddenly I feel as if I'm on familiar ground. To win this war, I need to unlock that attitude and to do that I first need to know my opponent. If I could find out why the little terror was so dead set on tunneling into my house, I might find a way to convince him to stop.

It's time to call on the experts.

I consulted three websites and all agree on the reasons why a woodpecker would ignore the twenty mature trees that are right behind him and choose to peck into my house instead. *The Audubon Society, The Cornell Lab of Ornithology* and my local environmental protection agency cite three possibilities: 1) He's foraging for bugs. 2) He's drumming to attract a mate. 3) He's drilling to make a nest for the winter.

Terrific. Are there bugs I need to worry about, too? Or is he actually working his way through the wall so that he can snuggle into the insulation which is much warmer than the trunk of any tree? Or am I just dealing with a horny little pecker who is drilling holes in my house to impress his girlfriend?

I take comfort in none of these.

It gets worse. Cornell makes it clear that time is of the essence in the woodpecker world and success is more likely if you stop him as soon as he starts.

Yep. I'm seven months and several holes too late for that.

*****

Well, I can't turn back the clock, but I can try some of the deterrents that have worked for others. I've discovered that it is possible to spend a lot of money on expensive "bird repellent systems" that move and make noise and reflect light in ways that are irritating or frightening to birds. But, I'm not convinced that I need to invest so heavily—not yet. Then, there are all kinds of sticky tape items that are much cheaper, but Cornell doesn't recommend these because the adhesive can get stuck in the birds' plumage which will make it difficult for them to fly. And I definitely want my little nemesis to fly. Away. Far away. At least as far as the sycamore tree.

I love, love, love the *BirdXPeller Pro* by Bird-X which sends out distress calls followed by predator calls. They have a little MP3 sample on their website and I tried it out on my boy. The woodpecker distress call got his attention, all right. He stopped pecking and his head darted in all directions. The distress call was followed by the call of the sharp-shinned hawk (!) which sent him right to the top of the linden tree. When I played it again, he couldn't fly out of the yard fast enough. It was my first small victory and the most fun I had all day.

The user reviews for *BirdXPeller Pro* on the website are very encouraging, but they are mostly written by people like farmers with big bird problems to solve.

I'm not there—yet.

*****

Well, my research has given me some direction, at least, and I am ready to engage. It will take a few days to implement a strategy and a few more to assess effectiveness. I cannot reveal details without risking humiliation but I will report back in full when I have achieved victory. Nothing short of unconditional surrender will do.

Game on!

Saving *Your* Life

- Write about an experience you've had with household pests—birds, bugs, rodents, etc.

- Find a specific bird that hangs out where you live. Identify it using the Cornell or Audubon websites and research its habits. Watch it for a while and write about your observations. Compare your observations to those of the experts.

- Pick another bird. Just watch it over time and write about it based on your own original research. You are the expert now!

- Find a birdcall online. Play it for your local birds and write about what happens. (It might be really cool!)

- Then, play it for your cat. This is just for fun.

- Invent a product that you think should exist. Make up a catchy name for it.

- Did anything else about this essay remind you of your own experiences? In your notebook, jot down one memory, thought or opinion that popped into your head as you were reading.

Woodpecker Wars
Episode Two
Brain Size Is Not a Factor

"Shoot the little bastard!"

This advice came to me in an email from a dear, old friend after he read the blog post about my ordeal in "Woodpecker Wars—Episode One." Just this and nothing more. Since I have always known him to be a compassionate and kind-hearted soul, I was stunned by his ferocity. Later, in another email, he qualified this testosterone-brimmed response by explaining how much he and his wife catered to the birds in their yard, how much enjoyment they got from them and how much he would do to stop any ungrateful little son of a bitch from pecking holes in his house. There is a line, you see. If you're a bird in his yard, don't cross it.

Come, instead, to my house, where my environmentally aware family will, with compassion and grace, let you peck all over us.

Another friend, driven to desperation by a persistent, home-wrecking woodpecker, indeed took out a contract on said bird, which, once carried out, stopped any and all future attempts at drumming and drilling by the hordes of other woodpeckers that hang out in her yard. The pecker was a renegade and an example to his flock, which took heed and is now quite content conducting its business in trees. My friend felt awful, but, even with a yard full of woodpeckers, she has not had a problem since.

A Facebook friend wrote I HATE WOODPECKERS!!!! on my page with such fierceness that I feared for his health. I offered a sympathetic ear, but I heard no more from him on the subject. I picture him sitting in a corner, red-faced, rocking back and forth, talking to himself and swatting aimlessly at the air. If you're reading this JA, reach out! Don't feel like you have to face it alone. We're here for you.

Woodpeckers are the most infuriating of birds, it's true. But we are the superior species with brains several times the size of theirs. We should be able to out-think them. I don't want to shoot this little feathery demon spawn, although I have had offers, and I wish that I could find a way to let him know that I have an executioner on call. Perhaps a letter with pictures of birds cut from magazines with little guns to their heads would scare him straight.

*****

This is not the first time that our house has gotten in a bird's way. All houses occasionally intersect with avian flight patterns. These, we assume, are unfortunate accidents, as we watch stunned birds gather their wits after a collision with a picture window or we clean up feathery corpses to keep the neighborhood cats from congregating.

But when perfectly normal-looking birds of assorted species throw themselves at the same window over and over again, for days on end, we question their motives and their sanity.

Our ordeal with the kamikaze sparrow started innocently enough. It sat in a tree just outside the bow window of our family room. It sang. It entertained friends. It watched TV through the window. And then, one day, instead of looking in to see what show was on, it started throwing itself into the window with increasing velocity. Over and over. Then it would resume its perch in the tree, as if to catch its breath or perhaps to get over its headache, and start in again. It was distracting and disturbing and it was making a mess of my window.

We bought a menacing plastic owl and put it on the windowsill. Nothing. So, I replaced the owl with my cat. Nothing, again, mostly because she ran away faster than the bird could fly. Then, I started hearing noises at the back of the house, too—this time a cardinal.

I was not surprised that silly little sparrows would act like this, but I expected more maturity from cardinals.

He sat on the railing of the deck and flew into the porch window. Repeatedly. He hovered for a moment in front of a pane, flew into it and bounced himself off the window and back to the railing. If it wasn't so disconcerting, it would have been comical.

Neither bird would stop and then one day they did. Almost simultaneously. I did nothing more than wait them out.

I later learned that birds see their own reflections in windows and believe that their territory is being threatened by other birds. This is a particular problem during nesting season when birds need to be protective of their space. So they are attacking what they think are other birds when what they are actually seeing is themselves.

Bird brains.

When my birds stopped torturing themselves, it was sudden and complete. I'm not sure if it was the end of nesting season or if the windows were just so dirty from their incessant crashing that they couldn't see their reflections anymore.

Solution to window crashing birds? Don't wash your windows. In fact, muddy them up. If the obsessed birds can't see a reflection, they won't attack. Keep in mind that they have teeny tiny little brains and that we can out-think them before breakfast. Take charge and use your head. Accept the fact that your cat will not help you.

*****

Someone once said that the best defense is a good offense, so my first line of defensive offense was to get my husband to climb a ladder and fill the woodpecker holes in the side of my house with wood putty. Brown, to match the trim. The *Cornell Lab of Ornithology* points out that the holes themselves are attractive to woodpeckers and let them know that we are open for business.

Well, we're closed now, damn it.

And, for insurance, I hung some aluminum plates to make noise and reflect the sun.

And that may have done the trick as it has been days now and we have been pecker free. See? Just a little research, a little perseverance, a little elbow grease, a little thinking like a bird— that's all it takes.

Keep your drumsticks crossed.

*****

I almost wish that he'd come back long enough for me to use the *BirdXPeller Pro* sample on him again. I got such enjoyment from actually communicating with the birds on their own level. It's unfortunate that I was making them fear for their lives, but it was really interesting to see them react. In "Episode One," I wrote about this device, made by Bird-X, which sends out bird distress calls as well as predator calls to frighten pest birds away. When I played the brief website sample for the birds in my yard, the effect on the woodpecker was immediate and dramatic.

But other birds reacted to it as well. At the sound of the distress call, a brave little tufted titmouse landed on the patio chair next to me, puffed out his gray, feathery chest and raised his wings, showing an orangey underwing that I'd never seen before. It was a valiant display of solidarity with the woodpecker, but as soon as the audio turned to the predator call, in this case a hawk, that baby was gone. So much for bravado.

And when the woodpecker returned, I went back outside and played the calls over and over again. At first, he was sort of on to me, and stuck around. But then, as if he couldn't take it anymore, he threw up his wings and took off. It took me a minute to notice the coterie of chickadees that had congregated on the lilac bush right next to where I was standing—like crows on a jungle gym. They were all turned to face me with their cute little black caps looking like helmets and their little chests puffed out like armor. As more and more of them landed in the bush, I backed away slowly and headed for the house, thinking about blackbirds and Suzanne Pleshette.

*****

That night I dreamed that I was the Backyard Queen. I wore an iridescent gown made from reflective mylar that went through several fittings so it that hugged my pear-shaped self, both top *and* bottom, with that fancy-dress-shop precision that even Queens can't find at the mall. My hair was done in a sophisticated upsweep, adorned with a seasonally appropriate crown of golden oak leaves and twigs. A fresh French-gel manicure and air-brushed makeup finished off the look so that when I stepped out the back door into the yard, all of nature could not help but take notice.

"The Queen is here," cried all the creatures of the backyard realm. "Long live the Queen!"

I stepped out of the shade and into the sun and music swelled from somewhere and my reflective dress seemed to burst into flames. Startled birds lifted in unison, and, when they were a safe distance, they broke into a song of admiration for the display. I was a benevolent Queen, they knew, provider of food and shelter and safety. But there were rules to be followed and lines to be observed. An occasional demonstration of dominance served as a necessary reminder of this. The creatures of the realm knew their places and respected my authority.

Except for the diminutive Downy Woodpecker, that cocky, rebellious little boy who was pecking holes in the side of my castle. He had stepped over the line and everyone in the yard knew it. They were waiting for a reaction from me which had to be decisive and swift. After thirty-six years as Queen, I knew how to maintain control of a realm.

His bad behavior was not to be ignored.

So I opened the gates to the cats that congregate just beyond the battlements on Mondays and Wednesdays when the piper purges the realm of wayward rats and I hung my *BirdXPeller Pro* from the eaves and tuned it in to a continuous loop of "Panicked Woodpecker/Hungry Hawk" and I filled in the holes in the shingles and I suspended aluminum pie plates from the gutters. I walked up to the corner of the castle and pulled from behind me my magical, animatronic hooty owl and held it up, up, up towards the wayward bird.

A hush fell over the yard. Birds and mammals and rodents and insects leaned in as far as they dared.

The Woodpecker gulped and then dug in. He was in it too deep to give up now. But his resolve wavered and I could see beads of sweat on his beak. The breeze blew the pie tins and the sun made them flash and glow like flame. The hawk call got louder and was reinforced by the live hawks in the trees. The distressed woodpecker call echoed in his brain like a nightmare. The owl stared, blinked and stared some more.

Despite his fear, the Downy resumed pecking the castle. Each time he pecked a new hole, it filled itself back in without explanation. But he continued to peck, peck, peck with wild abandon as if he had completely lost his mind, which, it is commonly believed, he had.

At my signal, the cats circled and began to climb. As they got closer and closer, his panic grew palpable. His breath came in gasps and his heart beat was visible.

And then it wasn't.

A victim of his own fear, he fell to the ground and was carried away by a cortege of cats.

Success was mine. It was, really, a battle of wits and mine won the day. The natural order of things was restored and a collective sigh of relief was heard across the realm. I stepped first into the shade to resume a non-reflective form and to acknowledge my subjects, accepting their appreciation and applause. And then, crisis terminated, I returned inside and left them all, once again, to their lives.

And they promised to leave me to mine.

*****

It was a dream, yes. But it came true. Well, sort of. The evil little hammering fool was gone. And I did it *without* killing him. All I had to do was to outsmart him. Fill in his holes. Really? Hang some shiny aluminum foil. Is that all? What is all this "woodpecker control" fuss about? I got all worked up over nothing! I used my head. And now he's gone! It was easy!

Almost too easy.

Hmm.

Saving *Your* Life

- Write about a problem that you thought you had figured out—but you didn't.

- Write about a pet that you trained. What methods did you use to teach that pet how to live with you?

- Write about one natural occurrence that we can't control that you wish we could.

- Use your imagination to invent a method or machine to stop, say, the rain from spoiling your picnic or the birds from pooping on your car or the snowstorm from coming on the weekend or whatever other natural event you want to adjust.

- Write about a dream you had that let you know that you were stressing out too much about something going on in your life.

- Write about a quickie solution you wasted your money on.

- Write about a fictional character who would be able to help you to deal with a problem that you're currently experiencing. (What would Atticus Finch do?)

- Write about a problem of yours as if it were a piece of fiction. Fairy tales are fun.

- Did anything else about this essay remind you of your own experiences? In your notebook, jot down one memory, thought or opinion that popped into your head as you were reading.

Woodpecker Wars
Episode Three
So This Is How It Ends
(With Apologies to Edgar Allan Poe)

'Twas a summer morning—early. Sun peeked through the blinds like pearly
Strands that cast their evanescent beams across my quiet floor.
As I slumbered, calm and cozy, waking slightly, feeling dozy,
Dreaming I might up and mosey, mosey to the coffee store,
Came a voice from deep within that whispered, "Screw the coffee store!

                Snuggle in and sleep some more."

But ere I snoozed another minute, came a sound with venom in it,
Like one that had tormented me relentlessly a year before.
"It cannot be!" I cried in terror. "Surely this is dreaming's error!
Imagination is the fiendish bearer of this threat of war!
A coffee-starved hallucination generates these sounds of war.

                Only this, and nothing more."

I rose and staggered toward the kitchen where I have a cupboard rich in

Caffeinated beverages to clear my head right to its core.

I popped a pod into the Keurig and found a spoon that soon would stir big

Circles that would help me cure ignescent fears that I deplore.

Extinguish, Coffee, if you can, these groundless fears that I deplore.

This I ask, and nothing more.

But coffee couldn't stay my thinking or keep my brain from quickly sinking

Back to those horrific days of helplessness a year before.

The morning's dream had got me going and quickly I descended knowing

I could not stop the thoughts from flowing. I had to let them have the floor.

These thoughts of terror would not leave me 'til I let them have the floor.

These are facts I can't ignore.

It was a lovely day last summer, when a little downy drummer

Landed on the linden tree that stately grew outside my door.

The yard was full of trees and birds and as I wrote I searched for words

To show my love of flocks and herds of land and sea and sky and shore.

I am a friend to all the beasts of land and sea and sky and shore.

So I was glad to add one more.

"Hello there little red-smudged Stranger! In this yard you're out of danger,
At least from rocks and children and the human hunters you abhor.
But nature's free to take its course here; weather is a fickle force here.
Predators have no remorse here. As such you must mind your store.
I will give you trees and freedom but you still must mind your store."

Welcome, friend. Be lost no more."

And so the little fleck-winged birdy surveyed tree homes—more than thirty—
Never seeming satisfied with any bough that he'd explore.
This summer of his discontent aroused in me a sentiment
Grown fearful of a temperament that could dismiss my sycamore.
What kind of bird would be unhappy pecking at a sycamore?

What new hell was I in for?

Soon his flight was growing frantic—his behavior, unromantic—
Pecking wildly at the trunks that for him no fulfillment bore.
As his path became erratic, the situation grew dramatic.
How could I be diplomatic with this wild insectivore?
"Go Fiend! This yard cannot delight a critical insectivore.

See what you can find next door."

I swear the earth stopped in its orbit but my brain could not absorb it
As the little downy bird's objectives from his beak did roar.
"You will soon regret this tension and your ill-bred condescension!
You, and your home by extension, presently will know the score.
When I return it will be you who'll wish we weren't keeping score.

    Until then, Sweetheart, mind your store."

For weeks I listened, ears tipped skyward, searching for a sign or byword—
Anything to let me know just when my foe would start his war.
Well before this altercation, we had planned a short vacation
Which increased my agitation and the dread that I forswore.
They never saw the depths of the anxiety that I forswore.

    And so they dragged me to the shore.

A week of sun and breeze and tide released a tension deep inside,
A tension wrought by visions of the bird imagination bore.
I deemed it fancy's evolution, my own twisted convolution,
And so I made a resolution. Forget the bird! Forget the war!
Birds don't talk, I told myself, and neither are they prone to war!

    Ah! Therapeutic is the shore!

But, though I came home tanned and rested, my resolution, yet untested,

Wavered uncontrollably as I approached my own front door.

And when I felt the doorknob turning, I sensed that loathsome dread returning

And suddenly I felt a yearning for the palliative shore.

Could I again breathe in the balm of balmy breezes at the shore?

No! Now I have to mind *my* store.

So in I went and set to reading a book about woodpecker breeding.

It said they pecked like maniacs to win the girls that they adore.

Soon I nodded, nearly napping, when suddenly there came a tapping,

As of someone gently rapping, rapping at my bedroom door.

Some late visitor entreating entrance at my bedroom door?

Wait! Where have I heard *this* before?

As I recalled that other poet, hell broke, but I didn't know it,

Releasing one small wingéd demon. Real! Not just a metaphor!

Not *in* my house as I implied, but on the clapboard just outside,

The muted sounds now amplified by vengeance borne from hell's dark shore.

It was the sound of havoc shrieking sharp like one from hell's dark shore.

And so in slipped this bird of war.

WOODPECKER WARS

I ran outside to chase the culprit perched as if up in a pulpit
Pecking holes in shingles, eaves and buttresses right to their core.
I knew after a brief inspection this called for my rock collection.
I hurled hard in his direction missiles that would tie the score.
But my aim was awful doing little that could tie the score,
                    So he smirked and pecked some more.

But I'm smarter than a bird-brain, and even though I had a migraine
I sought out information that would help me beat this canker sore.
Well-placed shiny objects vex him, strips of foil and pie tins hex him,
A predatory call deflects him, making space that he'll abhor.
All these things I put in motion making space that he'd abhor.
                    And soon I saw him nevermore.

Or so I thought—for came the winter. The holes were fixed with not a splinter
Showing how that little bastard tried to ruin my fine décor.
Anxiety grew in the springtime, as it was bird-on-the-wing time,
Yet all stayed well through pool-and-swing time, proving I had won the war.
By August I let down my guard declaring I had won the war.
                    He could never change the score.

Or so I thought—until this morning when without a word of warning
Percussive bird testosterone intruded and disturbed a snore.
It chills me to my deepest follicle, that this bird, so diabolical,
Wholly real and *not* symbolical, comes at will to peck once more.
And I am *not* the boss of nature. I'm just here to mind the store.
　　　　　　　　　　　Not just now, but evermore.

The End

Saving *Your* Life

- Write about a time when it became obvious to you that you are not the boss of nature.

- What else are we not the bosses of?

- Write about a time when you realized that you had to learn to live with something that you couldn't change.

- This poem is a parody. I have fit my words into the poetic structure of "The Raven," a famous and easily recognizable poem written by Edgar Allan Poe. I have worked to stay as close to the original in metrical pattern, rhyme scheme and stanza count as I possibly could. It took me a while, but I think I'm pretty close. It's a challenge, but a satisfying one. Try it. Start with just a single stanza of this poem and tell a story of you à la Poe.

- If you enjoy this exercise, find other poems to parody. Some I like are "Annabel Lee" by Poe, "The Tyger" by William Blake, "O Captain, My Captain" by Walt Whitman, "The Waking" and "My Papa's Waltz" by Theodore Roethke, "The Eagle" by Alfred Lord Tennyson, "Stopping By Woods," by Robert Frost and anything by Emily Dickinson. Or try a familiar song like "America the Beautiful" or "Winter Wonderland" or "Take Me Out to the Ballgame." Get a feel for the rhythm and then plug in your own words. It's fun!

- Did anything else about this essay remind you of your own experiences? In your notebook, jot down one memory, thought or opinion that popped into your head as you were reading.

Part Four
You *Can* Get There From Here

In the last chapter of his travelogue *The Innocents Abroad*, Mark Twain wrote, "Travel is fatal to prejudice, bigotry and narrow-mindedness and many of our people need it sorely on these accounts. Broad, wholesome, charitable views of men and things cannot be acquired by vegetating in one little corner of the earth all one's lifetime."

Of course, in Twain's era, physically moving from one place to another was required if one was to have any real concept of the lands beyond one's home. Now, we can see the world around us electronically with help from satellites, movies, TV, Skype, Google Earth, live-cams, streaming video, PBS, Anthony Bourdain, Go-Pros, drones, Rick Steves and so many other people and devices that bring the world to us. During The Gilded Age of the nineteenth century, Twain could not have anticipated The Digital Age of the twenty-first. Today, we can see it all without ever having to walk out the front door. Twain would have loved the gadgetry, but he would have hated the consequences.

That's because, with or without technology, his point is still valid today. Nothing compares to getting out of your house and your town and your comfort zone so that you not only can see, but also hear, smell, touch and taste the world for yourself. Put those senses to work. Meet people. Take a risk. Adjust the attitude. Interact. Enjoy. Discover. Learn. Change. Grow.

To broaden your horizons, you must physically step beyond them. That much hasn't changed.

But this doesn't mean that you have to stow away on a tramp steamer to Bora Bora to feel the benefits of travel. Exotic lands are indeed out there begging to be explored, but you don't have to go far from home to expand your world. You just have to go.

One thing's sure. Traveling, however you do it, results in a shipload of stories worth saving—and sharing.

Here are some of mine.

Caped Crusader

When I was teaching, I dreamed of being able to vacation in September. I imagined the fall to be the Holy Grail of travelers—cooler temperatures, fewer people, no kids. Of course, I couldn't know for sure as I had always been either a student or a teacher, spending Labor Day weekends laying out new clothes and packing lunches and stressing. Like most teachers, I pretty much missed out on September. Immersed in a new school year, I rarely had the time to enjoy (or even notice) the seasonal transition as summer's heat and humidity evaporated into the crisp, comfortable sweater-weather of fall. It seemed that one day I started school and before I knew it, there was snow.

Now that I have retired, everything has changed. As my former colleagues pack their book bags and head back to school, I pack a suitcase and head to Cape Cod.

Let me tell you, it was worth the wait.

I always loved the Cape. I camped in North Truro with friends back in the days when I did that sort of thing. We spent our time exploring the dunes on horseback, watching sunsets at Race Point, trying to find our way around a Coleman stove and flirting with the cute deck hands on the fishing boats that docked on MacMillan Pier in Provincetown. Later, the summer after we graduated from college, a dear friend and I rented a studio apartment in Hyannis. We spent our time beach-bumming, waiting tables, applying for teaching jobs and flirting with the cute deck hands on the tour boats that docked at the Hy-Line piers across the street. Once, I traversed Martha's Vineyard by bicycle with an old chum—but only once. After that we'd schlep down to Woods Hole where we could ferry over with the car. There we impersonated the Whimsies, hunted for famous people in the wilds of Chappaquiddick and took pictures of each other in Edgartown under Amity signs left behind by Steven Spielberg. On one trip we saw a frenetic performance by a then-unknown Cyndi Lauper at a little club called Hot Tin Roof—owned by James Taylor and Carly Simon. We danced, we laughed, we drank and we flirted—shamelessly.

Those were the days.

Without going into incriminating detail, let it be said that I am no stranger to the Cape. And as I settled down into a more responsible, adult lifestyle, the Cape was still a magnet as I discovered it to be more family-friendly than I ever cared to know when I was twenty-two. We brought the girls and their boogie boards and, over the years, body-surfed every beach along the Cape Cod National Seashore, staying in motels along Routes 6 or 6A until we had the means and the time to rent houses and pretend that we owned them.

And all of these adventures happened in the summer. Teachers have to pack all of their fun into the six weeks between the 4th of July and the middle of August. The rest of the time is pretty much sucked up in teaching—preparing, grading, thinking about preparing and grading, worrying, filling out forms, doing laundry and making lunches. The name of the game—play hard enough in August to remember it in September, because memories of fun and having a life are all you've got to hang on to once school starts.

*****

Now, much to the chagrin of my former colleagues, I look forward to the end of summer. Now in September, we rent a house and head toward the sea, like retired lemmings. We beat on, car against the current, making landfall on the Cape just as the last of the summer people are making their way home. We breathe a sigh of relief, like the locals, when the crowds drain south and west on Route 6 toward the mainland as we move east and north toward the tip of the continent.

And it is everything I imagined the Cape in September would be. Manageable traffic, free parking at the beaches, off-season discounted rental fees on the house, easy-to-get reservations at my favorite restaurants (if we need reservations at all), clear skies, tolerable temperatures, no lines at Arnold's or Box Lunch or Mac's Shack or Ben and Jerry's. And the beaches practically to myself. Writers' heaven.

We stay in Eastham (pronounced, I'm told, East-*Ham*) in a house that is one street from the bay. While I enjoy an occasional visit to Hyannis for old time's sake—a cruise by the Ocean Street Dock and my sweet little former apartment, a drive past the Kennedy compound where I used to ride my bike in hopes of meeting a cute Kennedy cousin, a stroll up Main Street past the place that once sold muffins the size of hedgehogs, a stop at the Hearth and Kettle for chowder or Baxter's for a quahog with a side of hungry seagulls—now I much prefer the more natural feel of the Lower Cape. Beach grass, dunes and piping plovers with their little white caps and teeny little matchstick legs say Cape Cod to me now.

Eastham is the gateway to the Outer (aka Lower) Cape. Yes, I know this sounds backwards, but if you think of Cape Cod as an arm, Hyannis is part of the bicep, Chatham is at the elbow, Orleans, Eastham, Wellfleet and Truro comprise the forearm and Provincetown is the hand and fingers. Hence, the further out on the Cape you travel, the further *down* the arm you go even though you are driving north and east. To leave the Cape, you must go back *up* the arm toward the shoulder even though you are now driving south and west. I doubt that this is the official explanation, but it is the one that helps me to remember that I go up cape to get to Falmouth and down cape to get to Truro, completely backwards from what you might expect.

People go to the Cape for different reasons. I have long since lost the urge for nightlife and shopping though there is plenty of it here. The party animal in me up and left the room years ago. The girls are grown now and with their childhood has gone the necessity for kid-friendly haunts like arcades and mini-golf and take-out fast food and trinket shops. It is a grown-up, more sedate Cape that I crave now—the thoughtful, creative Cape; the introspective, contemplate-one's-place-in-the-universe Cape; the sensory, inspirational, natural Cape; the Cape that calls me to it and talks to me when I get there. That one.

Now, it's all about the beach. And maybe the wine. And the nice restaurants, locally owned, not cheesy but not fancy, serving the freshest, sweetest scallops you are likely to find anywhere. And the galleries, rare in my suburbia but plentiful here, that prove that artists *can* make a living for themselves if the conditions are right and they are tenacious and the community is receptive. And one of the world's last remaining drive-in movie theaters, just so we don't forget where we came from. And the dunes, disrespectful of arbitrary boundaries, like roads, ever shifting and changing yet always there, happily-ever-after protected by the National Park Service. And the free spirits of all ages and persuasions. And the lighthouses. And the maritime history. And the stars. And the solitude. And the joy.

And, did I mention the beach?

If I had the money, I would buy myself a little house as close to Cape Cod Bay as I could get it. I would fill it with the work of local artists and artisans and eat locally caught seafood in every possible incarnation. Every morning I would sling a beach chair and bag (with a towel, some sunscreen, a notebook, two blue pens, a novel, a bottle of San Pellegrino and a plum) over my shoulder and I would walk to my office—whichever sandbar on the bay presented itself to me that day. I would write for three hours, walk for one and read for one more, come home to have lunch and then drive to the ocean side to watch the seals and search for smooth, white, oval stones to fill vases and lamps and baskets and then I'd sit down and write some more. I'd go out for dinner, at a restaurant where I had become a regular and people would know to watch for me and would worry and maybe call if I didn't show for too many nights running, and then come home to transcribe the day's writings on my laptop, polishing, editing and revising as I went. Then some wine and some late night TV (just to stay current) and off to bed to rest up for the next day's work. I would grow old and prolific and so involved in the intricacies of my work and the secrets of the universe that I would be oblivious to my growing fame and unaware of the deep affection with which readers held my words. I would live to write and would stay here until it was too cold to work from the beach. Then I would have the place shut up for the winter and fly south with the hummingbirds, counting the days until the earth traveled far enough through the year to reunite itself with a sun who would raise the temperature, melt the ice, calm the sea and allow me to once again step into my office on a sand bar in the bay.

But this is not likely.

So I content myself with an annual Cape Cod rental in the glorious and previously underappreciated month of September, the month when schoolteachers everywhere shake off the lethargy of the hot summer, rev up the engines of their lives and get back down to business. It is a cycle so ingrained that even retirement cannot alter it.

But what business is it to which the retired schoolteacher now gets down? And where? That, my friends, is limited only by the size of our dreams and the placement of our beach chairs.

Saving *Your* Life

- Think of a place to which you have returned many times. How have your activities changed over the years? What does this say about the place—and you?

- Are you retired? What old working habits or cycles were hard for you to change? What changes came easily?

- If you are working, fantasize about what your retirement will be like. Dream big. The sky's the limit.

- Now think a bit more realistically. What do you expect your retirement to really be like?

- In New England, autumn is a big deal. What is fall like for you? Describe autumn's seasonal traditions, environmental changes and the people's attitudes where you live.

- What is your favorite time of year for vacation? Why? Where do you go? Describe it for someone who's never been there.

- For some, the beach is a place of rest, renewal and inspiration. For others, it's a place of killer sharks, sunburn and sand sandwiches. Where do you fall on this spectrum? Support your stance with a description of your best/worst day on the beach.

- Many artists tell us how necessary solitude is to their work. Do you go out of your way to procure solitude? How do you deal with it when you get it?

- To write, I need solitude, quiet and large blocks of uninterrupted time. Do you crave quiet and natural sounds like waves and birds and wind or do you often feel the urge to fill the void with artificial sound like music or TV?

- Where is your Cape Cod?

- Did anything else about this essay remind you of your own experiences? In your notebook, jot down one memory, thought or opinion that popped into your head as you were reading.

The Wonder Horse of Saskatoon

Even though our trans-Canada road trip was thirty years ago, we are still the only hometown people I know who have ever been to Saskatoon.

It's pretty far. And pretty flat. And there's not much there to see. But, as memories of Canada go, this is one of my most persistent.

Like they say, someday you'll look back and laugh.

*****

I insisted that we go to Saskatoon. We were making our way across the continent via the Trans-Canada Highway, just for the fun of it. We had been on the road for several days in our zippy little 1980 Toyota Shoebox and had skirted the border for a while before shooting north—Sudbury, Sault St. Marie, Thunder Bay, Winnipeg. We were pretty good at traveling on the cheap—tent camping, driving ridiculous distances per day, eating bologna sandwiches and fighting off mosquitoes the size of dragonflies.

Just west of Winnipeg, near the town of Brandon, Manitoba, the Trans-Canada Highway splits. Route 16 heads north and west, toward regions that were, to me, adventuresome and exotic. Our plan was to stay on the lower fork, Route 1, into

Saskatchewan, through Regina, Moose Jaw and Medicine Hat. But I really, really, really, please, please, please wanted to take the other fork—North to Saskatoon! Huzzah!

I lost the argument for all kinds of practical reasons and we arrived in Regina, the pronunciation of which always makes me snort a little into my hand. We did enjoy a parade of Royal Canadian Mounted Police, the first I'd seen on this trip. This was a novelty but its entertainment quotient was low. It wasn't long before I used up my cache of Dudley Do-Right jokes, and my Nelle-on-the-tracks impression, which didn't have a lot going for it in the first place, wore thin. When even making up little rhyming songs about Regina wasn't fun anymore, I resumed my campaign to see the city of my dreams. One last chance. Route 11. Regina to Saskatoon. Two and a half hours. We will *never in our lives* come back here again. We are a mere two and a half hours away from the notoriety of being the only living people we will ever know who can say that they have been to Saskatoon, Saskatchewan, Canada. When my best Snidely Whiplash voice gave way to the slightly impeded sibilance of Sylvester the Cat ("Sufferin' Succotash! Take me to Saskatoon, Saskatchewan!"), we were turning onto Route 11.

It takes a good man to know when he's licked.

We had a brochure listing farms that welcomed campers and we found one just on the outskirts of the city. It was clean and reasonable and flat. We checked in, pitched our tent and made ourselves at home.

Then the wind shifted.

I should mention that this wasn't just any farm that we found. Oh no. Sure, they grew crops. After all, we were on the prairie here. But they also raised chickens. Thousands of them. You know those delectable, chewy little cubes of grayness that you find in every savory can of chicken noodle soup? Well here they were, still on the bone. And we suddenly found ourselves downwind of the "coop" which was a two-story, block-long condoplex full of clucking, flapping, pooping, ill-fated chickens. Welcome to Saskatoon. On a really hot day. Two thousand miles from home. With just our little tent.

Be careful what you wish for.

Our misery was apparent to the family. They empathized. So much so that they offered us a bed and dinner inside the big house. We jumped at the chance and had that tent down and back in the car before chicken #847C could cluck out the first verse of "O, Canada."

Dinner was baked chicken. It was quite—how can I put this—fresh.

And dinner-time conversation was lively. We sat with the farmer, his wife, two young-adult sons who worked the farm and obviously had a stake in it and a couple of younger boys. They had all kinds of questions and opinions about American politics. They knew all of our leaders and their policies and they weren't shy about expressing their views. We were impressed by the extent of their knowledge and understanding of American affairs and embarrassed by the fact that we couldn't reciprocate when the topic turned to Canadian politics. Our ignorance of their affairs was not unexpected, and they filled us in on the need-to-know information as they discussed the chasm between what they called the Two Canadas—the western, agricultural, working people's Canada and the eastern, elitist, intellectual, whiny Canada which usually got its way because the population was denser there. Talk of secession was served up with dessert.

Then came the offer from which romantic vacation memories are made.

"There's a good piece of daylight left. Would you like to take the horses out for an after-dinner, sunset ride?"

Hell, yeah.

I couldn't remember the last time I had ridden a horse, but the family assured us that these were gentle and well-trained. The boys saddled them up and pointed us west.

"Head on down this road until you get to the fence that marks the property line. Can't miss it. Then just turn around and come back. The horses know the way."

Yes. Yes, they did.

Off we went. Rogers and Evans. Chaplin and Goddard. Wild Bill and Calamity Jane. Two happy travelers just a'headin' into the sunset. Feelin' good.

Happy Trails to us.

The road was wide and straight. And flat. On either side were fallow fields, so we could see for miles in all directions, as if we were in the middle of the ocean. New Englanders don't understand this concept of flatness. We think that if we can see a few hundred feet before the road curves or a tree appears or a hill rises to break the view that we're out in the open. Prairie flatness, though, is miles and miles and miles of no curves, no trees, no hills. There are no obstacles in your path. There's also nowhere to hide. As we traveled through the plains, I vacillated between feeling totally free and frighteningly vulnerable.

But I wasn't worried about any of that now. The evening was

warm and we were together and the sun was setting in the west and our beautiful brown horses knew the way. These horses were born to be ridden and they seemed to know what to do with these two greenhorns from back east. Their gait was easy and rhythmical. We barely needed to hang on.

Then we reached the property line.

They were right. You can't miss it.

If we were in a movie, the following scene would begin with a tight close up on my horse's eye, perhaps winking for the camera, and a shot of his nose coming even with the fence and giving it a ritualistic nudge. Then the camera would pull back, and the editing would quicken as John (yes, his name was John) reared as if stung, spun around like a dog with a flea on his ass, and broke into a full gallop.

You bet your ass I was hanging on now.

I grabbed the reins and pulled back on them as hard as I could. I yelled WHOA! I thought that the horse would respond to my command because I was the rider, albeit a rider of limited experience, and he was a "well-trained" horse. He did not. In fact, my entreaty seemed to make him run faster. I had a vision of all those Yosemite Sam cartoons where he yells WHOA and the horse pays him no mind whatsoever. They were funny. This was not.

Two things were suddenly clear. 1) I was on a runaway horse. 2) I was about to die.

Well, I wasn't giving in so easily. Since it was obvious that there was no stopping John, I focused all of my energy on not falling off. I pushed down on the stirrups and pressed in my knees in an effort to stabilize myself and not fly off into space. I think I even grabbed his mane at one point just to keep myself upright. Sure, pull his hair. That should calm him down. I felt like I was flopping all over the place and would certainly hit the ground any minute and smash to a million pieces. I couldn't keep this up much longer. I closed my eyes and yelled to my husband what I was certain were to be my last words.

"My mother is going to KILL you!" I tried to say.

But all that came out was, "MAAAAAAAAAAMAAAAAAAAAA!"

There was nothing else I could do but hang on for dear life. I was terrified, but, miraculously, I stayed in the saddle. To this day, I don't know how.

John ran and ran. I felt as though he would never stop.

And then he did.

When I opened my eyes I saw that we were back in the barn, right where we started from—in the stall with the name "John" burned into the wood over the window. He was calmly eating hay and waiting for me to get the hell off his back.

I heard laughter coming from the split-rail fence just outside the barn. I dismounted, checked my pants to make sure they were dry and hobbled outside.

There was the entire family, just a-settin' on the fence, waiting to welcome us back. TV reception's not great out here. I wondered if I was their evening's entertainment.

"So, how was it bein' in the saddle again? Fun?"

It was like asking a Titanic survivor if she enjoyed her little boat ride.

I feigned control. "The first half was great. The ride back was a bit of a challenge. But I handled it." I felt a lump rise in my throat. I fought back the tears. Then I lost it.

"My life passed before my eyes! I could have been killed! He's wild! Why did you put me on that runaway monster???"

I felt my husband's calming arm around my shoulder. I gathered my wits and after a moment began breathing normally again.

"Why, John's not a monster!" said the farmer's wife. "He's the calmest guy in the barn. He just thought he was doing what he was supposed to be doing."

"Scaring the shit out of me?"

"Naw. Taking you for a joyride. You see, the boys ride that pair out to the property line every night. They walk out slow and enjoy the sunset and then they touch the fence and race back. It's a game. Winner is the first one back into his stall. It gives 'em all a chance to blow off steam and feel the wind in their hair."

Wind in my hair? I have a blow dryer for that.

"Well, you could have warned us. I could have been…"

"You did just fine. John would never have thrown you. He'd've stopped if he didn't feel like you were in control. He's a wonder that way! Now let's head inside. I'll make you up the bed in the spare room."

It took me a bit to settle down to sleep, but once I did I dreamed that I was a trick rider in a circus. I wore white tights and a red tutu and I twisted myself around the neck of a galloping horse to pick a handkerchief up off of the ground with my teeth. Then, for our finale, the horse flipped me up on his bare back where I stood in triumph with arms outstretched as we raced around the ring to thunderous applause. What a team!

*****

Over thirty years have passed and I haven't been on a horse since. There are some experiences that are just meant to be your last even if you don't know it at the time.

And, by the way, if you have ever been to Saskatoon, please don't tell me.

Saving *Your* Life

- What have you done that you absolutely know you will never do again? Describe the experience so that someone else can appreciate the significance of the event.

- What have you done that no one else you know has done? There must be at least one thing that is totally yours. Dig it up and describe it.

- Have you ever thought about where your food comes from? Trace an origin, real or fictional, of the next thing you eat.

- Pick one memorable travel story and write it down for others to enjoy.

- Where have you always wanted to go? Why? Plan the trip.

- What childhood cartoon characters still make their way into your conversations today? Pick one and explore its effect on you.

- Are you conversant in the politics of another country? If so, pick one thing that you think Americans should know and explain it.

- Are Americans in general uninformed about world affairs? Why? What should we do about it?

- Describe a time when you were sure you were a goner.

- Did anything else about this essay remind you of your own experiences? In your notebook, jot down one memory, thought or opinion that popped into your head as you were reading.

Olive Tree, Very Pretty

In Italy, plants and trees grow everywhere. Most of the land that we saw as we traveled around the country is cultivated—not forests or swamps or thickets or the wild, natural growth that we see driving through New England, but things in neat rows, often for as far as the eye can see. It seems that every inch of arable Italian land is nurtured—and arable land can be anything from a huge expanse of sunny hillside to an errant patch of dirt by the side of the road. Where there is no dirt, as in many of the hilltop towns that are covered from edge to edge in stone, there are window boxes and planters and pots. There will be growth here. Tradition demands it.

The Italian sun shines ceaselessly. It is a perfect climate for acres of sunflowers, towering cypress trees, bushels of tomatoes and peppers and zucchini and aromatic bunches of basil, groves of lemon trees for potent limoncello, kilometers of grape arbors for perfect Italian wines and rows and rows and rows of squatty, clipped, carefully spaced trees. Many, especially in Sicily, are pistachio trees, but most bear the green jewels of Italian cuisine—olives.

Growing up, I was never much of an olive fan. I liked the black ones—still do—but the green ones from the supermarket were too salty, too pungent, too slippery, too small. And they always had that stupid red pimento stuck in there where the pit used to be. They looked festive enough arranged with black olives and little pickles in the divided crystal dish that my mother put out for company, but they tasted awful. Even now, when I make a pickle and olive tray for family gatherings, those green olives are left behind to be scooped back into the briny jar after everyone has gone.

They are not the olives I learned to love in Italy.

Olives in Italy are treated like a delicacy long before they ever make it to the table or, if they are destined to become olive oil, to the press. I thought this the first time I saw an olive grove. The trees, some of which are hundreds of years old, are treated with respect. They are planted with deference to their needs and, in return, they grow strong and can bear fruit through several human lifetimes.

Olives love the sun. Long, hot Mediterranean summers are perfect for them. But they must be planted and pruned to maximize their sun exposure. Italian olive growers are sensitive to this. Rarely did I see trees touching each other—even the really old ones. They are spaced so that each tree inhabits its own spot, drinks from its own ray of sunshine, casts its own distinct shadow and has plenty of room to grow. Twisty, gnarly trunks give way to branches that reach out first horizontally and then curve vertically in an effort to bare each leaf, each blossom, each olive to the sun. Olive leaves look silvery, especially from a distance, and they seem to reflect the light even as they absorb it. Caretakers help this along by pruning from the center, taking out the tallest, most vertical branches because they cast shadows and steal sunlight from the rest. This kind of pruning makes mature trees look like great branchy bowls full of olives or giant cupped hands full of sunshine. If you put your wrists together at your pulse points, flatten out your palms like a table and then arch your fingers up towards the sun, you'll see exactly what I mean.

Sometimes, especially in Sicily, we would see olive trees on their sunny hillsides keeping company with grape arbors for the good sun and sheep for the grassy grazing land. Perched like paintings, these displays, accented by a deep blue sky dotted with fair-weather clouds and, if we were lucky, a glimpse of the sea, have become, for me, indelible souvenirs of my travels. They remind me that beauty exists. Somewhere. Always. All we have to do is find it and look at it.

And, wherever we find beauty in Italy, in the middle of it all is probably a work of art or an olive tree.

On our travels, we learned that olives, like grapes, have different flavors and textures and that olive oils, like wines, taste different depending on where they're grown. We taste-tested in a shop with crusty bread and oil in dipping bowls and a knowledgeable instructor. I was amazed at the differences among the oils in body and aroma and personality. I bought two different tins of rather expensive oils which I could never bring myself to open. They sit today, decoratively, on my kitchen counter, well past their expiration dates. I couldn't have my Sicilian olive oil and eat it, too. So I just have it.

We learned to eat olives as appetizers served in bowls before our meals instead of bread. Plump, shriveled, three shades of green, two shades of red and one of brown, marinated, fresh, sweet, pungent, oily—we ate them all, spitting the pits out like watermelon seeds into our cupped hands. We knew that, like most of what we ate in Italy, these olives had most likely been grown only a mile or two from where we sat and that made all the difference. We had never enjoyed eating olives so much in our lives. It wasn't long after our return home that we were thrilled to be once again served a bowlful of olives as an appetizer. It was Becco's in New York City that honored the olive so and we ate them like candy and reminisced. Since my memory of the flavors has faded some since then, it might be time for another journey, to New York, anyway. We'll pretend.

I had no idea until I saw them for myself that olives and their trees had such personalities. It is no wonder to me now that we offer their branches as symbols of peace and reconciliation. Sun-loving, ageless and prolific, the trees live for centuries. If only the peace we purport to crave could last a fraction of that time.

Many olive trees that I saw could have been planted when settlers were first finding their way to the New England that I live in now or when the ink was drying on our Declaration of Independence or when George Washington was standing at the helm of the new country. Individual trees have been there as long as we, as a nation, have been here. They know things.

And they know people. John Keats and I might have eaten olives grown from the same tree. Or perhaps I ate from the same olive branch as Michelangelo. Or Galileo. Or the last of the Medici. Or Enrico Caruso. Or Sophia Loren. Or George Clooney.

Imagine.

The lovely little olives that have grown on the same trees on the same land for centuries remained a mystery to me until I traveled to where they are. They don't keep secrets, but they only seem to reveal them to those who come to see for themselves.

And so, now, there is growth here, too.

Saving *Your* Life

- What has your experience been with olives? Many people only acquire a taste for them as adults. What's your olive story?

- What food have you discovered on your travels that has surprised you?

- What foods, for you, define a time or place?

- What is the oldest living thing you've ever seen?

- Do you have a favorite tree? If so, write about why it is special for you.

- Do you generally not pay much attention to trees? If not, pick one that is nearby and watch it for a while. What is unique about it? What has caught your eye? What kind of life might it have had up until now?

- Think of one thing that you have seen in your travels that has had a lasting effect on you. Describe it and what you have learned from it.

- What picture in your head reminds you of the beauty that exists in the world?

- Did anything else about this essay remind you of your own experiences? In your notebook, jot down one memory, thought or opinion that popped into your head as you were reading.

And the Birds Still Sing

Traveling in Europe requires constant adjustment. After two weeks in sunny and sometimes sweltering Italy, we flew over the Alps from Venice to Munich where it was 55° and raining. People were wearing wool scarves and parkas. I didn't pack a parka. It was June, for God's sake.

We were meeting up with a tour group later in the day, so we arrived in time to have this morning to ourselves. There was someplace nearby that we were compelled to visit before starting on a carefree tour of Austria and Switzerland. Before slipping into the world of the von Trapps and Mozart and ski bums and jet setters and schnitzel and chocolate and oompah bands and nice white wines, we knew there was another place that we needed to see.

From our hotel in Munich, it took us two trains and two buses to get to the town of Dachau—Bus 54 to the Giselastraße, Train U3 to Train S2 and, finally, Bus 725 to our destination. The German public transportation system is clean and efficient and, like everything else here, means business. The train station—spotless, graffiti-free, austere—is meant to move people, not entertain them. It is well-marked and straightforward and built to perform. The trains arrive on time and depart on the dot. Unless you arrive early, the doors will close in your face.

I know this from experience.

The time listed on the schedule is not the time that the doors close. It is the time that the train leaves. There is no discussion on this. And there is no opening a door once it has closed, even though the train will not move for another minute. It is your problem if you are left standing on the platform and not in the car. In Germany, we discovered, things are quite punctual. Presence, not arrival, at the appointed time is expected. In other words, to Germans, punctuality means arriving early. If you arrive right on time, then you are late.

The stops here have names of many syllables— Mammendorf, Donnersbergerbrücke, Kleinberghofen, Schwabhausen. On our first day in Germany, this was a novelty. It was a game to try to pronounce them before we passed the signs. Sometimes we could, but only sometimes.

We made our way from bus to train to train to bus. As it was Saturday, most of our conveyances were uncrowded and seats were plentiful. But Bus 725 to Dachau was crammed full. For the first time on this excursion, we had to stand. People were quiet and well-behaved even though they were pressed up against one another. They were bundled against the cold, so there was little in the way of actual, physical contact. Still, we sensed by people's expressions that the proximity issues here were uncomfortable for them. (For us, this was nothing compared to the squishier, sweatier, more-the-merrier, skin-exposed subways of Rome.) But more important than comfort was the significance of the destination. We all had someplace important to go, someplace somber, someplace unspeakable. Thinking about *that* invalidated our discomfort.

ARBEIT MACHT FREI. The large, metal, block-style capital letters scream to us from the entrance gate as we approach the Dachau Memorial.

"Work will set you free."

The concept is preposterous. Work that you love might set you free, but work that is forced upon you has the opposite effect, no matter how much the oppressor insists to the contrary. But to make the ridiculous assertion, to insist that it is true and to back it up with muscle and intimidation instead of logic, instantly reveals a culture of torment and persecution. Schoolyard bullies all grown up. It is so because we say it is so.

You will do as you are told.

I feel this sensation as soon as I enter the camp—the pressure, the uncertainty, the terror of what life here must have been. *Arbeit Macht Frei.* It sets a tone, even all these years later, even to tourists who come and go at will and who do not fear for their lives.

Resistance is not an option. You will obey.

We pass through the gate which is set in a tunnel formed by the walls of the Jourhaus, the former office building of the *Schutzstaffel*—the SS, the most dangerous and brutal of the Nazi forces. The building and gate create an imposing entrance, one that, even now, a visitor is right to think twice about before passing through.

Dachau stands today much as it did when it was used by the Third Reich as a concentration camp in the 1930s and 40s. Many buildings are gone, new ones have been built and old ones have been either preserved or repurposed, but the space is configured now the same as it always has been and it doesn't take much imagination to picture the place as a working camp. It is spotless and quiet. And its ghosts are everywhere.

We enter through the gate along with our fellow passengers of cramped Bus 725. Once inside the camp, it hardly seems that there are enough of us to have so crowded that bus. As we disperse into the expanse before us, we seem small and far apart and detached. This is fine with me. I need all the space I can get to take this in. The fewer people who dot my view, the easier it is for me to see the ghosts and let them tell their stories.

The day is drizzly and cold, the sky an unobstructed steel grey. I am ill-prepared and underdressed. I can't get warm and the dampness is getting under my skin, chilling me from the inside out. I look at the thin walls of the barracks and wonder how prisoners managed the cold German winter when I am uncomfortable here in the middle of June. It occurs to me that many of them didn't. I pull my light jacket closer, tug the hood up on my head against the rain and move on.

The camp is a perfect rectangle, twice as long as it is wide. Everything lies in straight lines and right angles—orderly, regimented, imposing. Grass and trees are within sight, generally beyond the barbed-wire fences and guard towers. But the initial view from the entrance is dominated by low buildings and large expanses of flat, paved or gravel grounds. It is a place that is easy to patrol. One would be hard-pressed to fall out of line inconspicuously here. There seems to be nowhere to hide.

Dachau was the first of what became an expansive system of Nazi concentration camps. It was established in 1933 and operated without interruption until it was liberated by American soldiers in 1945. It was considered a training camp for the SS and is not known for the mass exterminations that happened in death camps like Auschwitz and Treblinka. But the heaps of emaciated corpses found here by the liberators at the end of the war tell their own story. Some forty-thousand murders took place here in its twelve years—a huge number, yet just a fraction of the lives stolen during Hitler's reign.

I learn all of this as I walk through the Permanent Exhibition, a detailed, thoughtful and informative presentation of artifacts and panels displaying historical text and pictures. It is housed in what was formerly a maintenance facility at the south end of the camp. I read of the rise of Hitler, the social and cultural elements that allowed his power to flourish, and the history of Dachau and other camps like it. I think of human nature and the fragility of society and the notion that Americans hold that we are somehow immune to this sort of deception. We are too sophisticated to be so duped, too smart to be so manipulated, too secure to be so endangered, too humane to be so coerced. Vigilance is unwarranted. Democracy as we know it is our birthright. We are chosen. We are safe. This could never happen again. To anyone. Least of all to us.

Then, as I read the rhetoric on the wall, I shudder at its familiarity.

The maintenance building spans nearly the width of the south end of camp, a single-story, pitched-roof structure with arms reaching north at right angles on both sides. In the aerial pictures, it looks like the head table at a business luncheon. Inside, in the rooms housing the Permanent Collection through which we just walked, prisoners were admitted to the camp. In places where we stood, they were stripped, examined, decontaminated, humiliated and robbed of their belongings and their sense of individuality. The prisoner bath areas, also in this building, became sites of painful and debilitating punishments.

Stretched along behind this building is the camp prison.

This strikes me as a redundancy.

We are unsettled as we leave the Maintenance Building. The lessons we have learned here are not new to us, but standing in this camp and breathing its air somehow gives them a new urgency. We walk back out into the cold mist and head towards the roll-call area, a huge expanse of gravel between the Maintenance Building and the prisoner barracks. The sidewalk in front of the building guides us first to the International Memorial Sculpture. It sits perched on the top of a cement wall that stands about as tall as me. From there the sculpture rises up another several feet, a black metal tangle of what looks like a barbed wire fence. I have to step back a bit to see that the sculptural elements snarled in this fence are human—horizontal, fleshless, featureless, twisted bodies with fingers and toes splayed to resemble the ubiquitous barbs. Their torment is complete, their agony inescapable. I stand in the rain and look up at the sculpture for a long time.

We move further into the camp.

The original barracks are all gone. Two replicas, one on either side of the camp road, have been built to give visitors a sense of the crowded conditions and the complete lack of privacy that prisoners endured. Many of these prisoners, especially at first, were political—unionists, Nazi opponents, communists, uncooperative clergy. Homosexuals, Jews, gypsies and Jehovah's Witnesses came later and they died not from asphyxiation in the gas chamber, but from overwork, beatings, shootings, medical experiments, starvation, punishment, cruelty, and diseases like typhus that breed in deplorable living conditions.

There were thirty-four original barracks, seventeen on each side of a poplar-lined road. The places where they stood are today represented by carefully measured and spaced raised beds bordered by wooden ties and filled with gravel. Each has a marker displaying its number. As I walk down the road, I feel the ghosts emerging from invisible barracks and marching south into the open area for roll call. Over two hundred thousand prisoners used this road at one time or another during the camp's existence. For many of them, it was the last road that they would ever walk.

We work our way north towards the back of the camp. The rain has stopped but the sky has not cleared and there is no warmth in the air. I only have two pairs of shoes with me on this trip, so I try hard to avoid the puddles that have formed in the road. Back here are several memorials and, oddly, a working Carmelite Convent on the grounds of a former recreation area built by prisoners for the pleasure of the SS. We will come back this way and give each area our attention. But we have another place to go first.

Off to the left, separated from the carefully measured camp rectangle by trees, is the crematorium. The old one, a single oven in a little chalet of its own, proved inadequate for the job it was called upon to do here, so new ones were built. They still weren't enough, even working around the clock, as evidenced by the heaps of corpses waiting their turn when the allies came in 1945. I saw a picture of one of those mounds of bodies piled up in front of the crematorium. I realize now that I stood in that exact spot.

We walk in silence through the rooms of the brick building with the oversized chimney—the ovens, the decontamination chambers, the fumigation cubicles, the single gas chamber with the word *Brausebad*—shower—printed in block letters over the entrance. This chamber was not used for mass executions, we are told. It was a prototype and so it was used on a much smaller scale than those of the larger death camps. Standing inside it, I sense the ghosts, just the same. There is plenty of death here to go around.

The chill on the back of my neck as I stand in this chamber is not from the cold.

We leave the crematorium area, pass back into the camp proper and explore the memorials at the north end of the rectangle. We pass a life-sized bronze statue of a man standing on a cement pedestal that resembles a gravestone. He is thin with a bald head, sunken eyes and hollowed-out cheeks. He wears a shapeless overcoat that is too big and seems to weigh him down, pants that are too long and shoes that are too heavy. His hands are plunged into the pockets of his coat as he looks resignedly off into the distance. Behind him is a grove of trees, green and vibrant, and in front of the pedestal is a bowl of pink and white begonias. The pedestal itself is set on tastefully designed marble pavers anchored in white gravel. It is respectful, tasteful and, in its own way, beautiful.

Carved into the pedestal are the words *"Den Toten Zur Ehr Den Lebenden Zur Mahnung."*

To Honor the Dead. To Warn the Living.

There are three chapels on the grounds. The Russian Orthodox Chapel, built in 1995 by Russia to honor the Soviet prisoners who died here, is a small hexagonal log structure with a steeple topped by an onion dome and an Orthodox cross. It is raised up on a little hill and set in a grotto of green trees and grass. The blue background of the painting of Mary and Jesus above the door stands in lovely human contrast to the natural elements that surround it. The spot offers visitors a moment of serenity and natural beauty and I welcome the relief that it provides.

The next memorial that we reach is the *Evangelische Versöhnungskirche,* the Protestant Church of Reconciliation, built in 1967. Offered as an apology by the Protestant clergy for not being an adequate obstacle to the rise of the Third Reich, its design is unique, paradoxical. Outdoor stairs bring us around and down into a walkway with a cement roof that only partially encloses the tunnel it forms. Cement walls are grey and unadorned and create a path underground into the church that is oddly curved, like walking into a conch shell. Once inside, we stand in a sanctuary stripped of all the trappings we might expect to find. Or so we think. They are there, but as symbols, metaphors. We have to stand there for a moment before they appear to us, like images that emerge when our eyes adjust to a dark room. The single rose on the round cement table that serves as the altar, the cylindrical cement pedestal that supports a single white pillar candle, the splash of red on single narrow window, the rough-hewn, backless benches, the edge of the cross that seems to burst out of the confines of the great, grey wall, the suggestions of curves and a deliberate avoidance of right angles. This building that begins as a shapeless, grey monstrosity ends as poetry. It, too, sounds a warning and provides a place to meditate and remember.

The Roman Catholic Chapel of Christ's Mortal Agony, built in 1960, stands at the very center of the north end of the camp. It is the point of the vee created by the parallel lines of poplar trees that line the camp road. Five stories of stonework form a cylindrical chapel that comes around only just so far on each side without coming to a close, open and welcoming. Inside is an altar and on the stone wall behind this altar is an enormous cross. An umbrella-like metal roof encloses the chapel from the top and supports a huge sculptural crown of thorns. The curved structure is a relief from the regimented angularity of the camp, the thorns a reminder of the persecution and torment of which humanity is capable. Reverence. Remembrance. Vigilance.

These three memorials suggest remorse, support, unity. They are uplifting and poetic and hopeful and they relieve, at least a little, the doubt a visitor might entertain about a human race that could allow such brutality in its midst. The Jewish Memorial, however, plunges us back into the harsh reality that there is no way to mitigate what happened here. This memorial is a right triangle, built of black stone and open at one end. There is a ramp, bordered by wrought iron fences shaped like barbed wire, which descends into the maw of the memorial and underground. There is a fence at the opening with gates, displaying Stars of David, that one passes through to enter into a stone enclosure. Above the entrance appears a passage in German from Psalm 9:21. "Put them in fear, O Lord, that the nations may know themselves to be but men."

Inside is stone, bare except for two memorial plaques—one written in Hebrew and other in Hebrew and German. It is dark inside and I feel as though I have walked down into an oven. At the far end of the structure, opposite the entrance at the room's lowest point, is a vertical stripe of light-colored stone that starts at the floor and rises several feet up the wall to an opening in the roof. There is a puddle on the floor beneath it from the morning's rain. Projecting from the opening in the roof is a stone menorah. One can't help but look up at it. Light. Hope. Even here.

As we near the end of our visit, we pass by areas that are lush and green and landscaped lovingly with yews and begonias and pachysandra. One such enclave of yews encloses a circular green mound, a grave of ashes. Behind the mound stands a small stone monument. Carved on it are a menorah, a Star of David and the words "Do Not Forget" in German, Hebrew and English. In front of the mound is a marble slab that says, "Grave of thousands unknown." Nearby, another grave of ashes has two crosses, a wood-hewn one standing at the back and a marble one resting on the ground across the top. The stone reads, "Grave of many thousands unknown."

Though many visitors pass by here, it is quiet except for the sound of footsteps in the gravel. People are moved by what they see and they treat the area with respect. In the silence, I am aware for the first time of the sounds of birds in the trees. This corner of the camp is lightly wooded and many birds make their homes here. Their songs are lively and my spirits are lifted to think that nature could bring such relief to a place like this.

I walk a bit further toward a wooded area with a path leading to a little clearing marked by a stone. The path is crisscrossed with the exposed roots of trees so I need to watch my step. A cement wall, streaked with ivy, sits perpendicular to the end of path. At the base of the wall, the undergrowth, full and green, creeps towards me. The chatter of the birds is everywhere and it is a welcoming sound. I stoop to read the marker and learn that this little garden path has taken me to an execution range. Prisoners were lined up against that wall and shot—not six feet from where I stand. The blood ditch at the foot of the wall is mostly obscured now by the plants that serve as groundcover.

And, still, the birds sing.

And they will continue to sing—even when our behavior proves us undeserving of their song.

History shows that while evil lurks among us and sometimes takes control, its authority, undermined by its own cowardice, never lasts. Still, it lies in wait beneath the surface, feeding on our ignorance and our fears. Like a vampire, evil cannot long survive in the daylight, so it does its damage in darkness and disguise, ambushing humanity at its weakest moments. Ultimately, it is overcome by the brave, but only after its damage has been done. Then we grieve and build memorials like this one and cry "Never again" until our complacency and our self-involvement and our witlessness and our fear feed it again and the cycle continues.

I learned that day at Dachau that nature, left to its own devices, will cover our mistakes. The trees will grow. The flowers will bloom. And the birds will sing. But nature will not take away our naïveté, our sense of entitlement, our fear of diversity or our capacity for brutality. It will not keep us from ignoring the truth or trusting the wrong people. Hitler did not come into power on his own. It took a whole world to make him—and then to take him down. What a price we paid for our complacency, our ignorance, our fear.

We can fortify ourselves by learning all we can, by reaching out, by standing up. The lessons we need are all around us—in history, in literature, in language, in travel, in music, in art, in math and science—in the things that teach us to see ourselves, to appreciate differences, to understand the workings of the world around us, to think critically and to detect and defeat malevolence.

Knowledge validates and reinforces for us the necessity of vigilance. It encourages us to see beyond ourselves and to incorporate others into our world view. It builds in us confidence and wisdom and discretion. It makes us better. It makes us brave.

And maybe someday, if we are wiser, when the birds sing, as they will, we can feel as if we are worthy of their song.

Saving *Your* Life

- Traveling is a learning experience, even when it is uncomfortable. Write about a place that taught you a lot even though it may not have been pleasant.

- What historical site would you most like to visit? Write about why this spot is interesting to you. What would you hope to gain by going there?

- Do you think it is a good idea to preserve sites where terrible things happened? Would you encourage people to go to them? Why or why not?

- Sometimes, the best way to give others a feeling of a place is to describe it in details that are as specific and concrete as you can make them. Choose a place that has affected you emotionally and try to get the feeling of it across to a reader with lots of specific, sensory details.

- People of my generation are the children of those who experienced World War II first hand. In my case, they didn't talk about it much and it never occurred to me to ask—then. Now, of course, they are all gone and it is too late. Think about an historical event that your parents lived through. If you are lucky enough to still have them, ask them about what they remember and how this event affected them. If, like mine, your parents are gone, do a little research into the event and its overall effect. Then, write a description of the event from the point of view of your parents—real or as you might imagine it.

- What can you learn about a city from its mass transportation system (or lack of one)? Choose a city you have visited and describe how you got around. What impression did this give you of the city and its inhabitants?

- Write about a time when you were comforted by nature.

- Write about a time when you were a victim of discrimination. What were the circumstances? How did you handle it? How did it affect you afterwards?

- Write about a time when you discriminated against someone else. What were the circumstances? Why did you do it? How do you feel about it now?

- What fields of study do you think would make the world a better place? Why do you think so?

- What one historical event do you think everyone should learn about and remember? How would this knowledge improve our world?

- Everything I know about Dachau I learned from my visit. You can learn about it from a very comprehensive website that is managed by the Memorial itself. Visit this website (https://www.kz-gedenkstaette-dachau.de/index-e.html) and take a virtual tour of the camp. Write about the experience.

- Did anything else about this essay remind you of your own experiences? In your notebook, jot down one memory, thought or opinion that popped into your head as you were reading.

How to Pack: A Primer for the Organizationally Challenged

I am not exactly what you'd call a seasoned traveler. I've taken plenty of vacations, but traveling is different. Vacations are when you pack up everything in your house and take it to another house for a week or two, and then pack it all up again and take it home. Vacations take you to predictable, relaxing places like the lake or the beach. Vacations require you to drive so that you can bring the coffee maker, a couple of lawn chairs, five pairs of shoes and the cat. Vacations are a lot like being home, except with sand and twice as many wet towels.

Traveling, on the other hand, is a much less casual endeavor. Traveling involves flying and/or moving from place to place within an allotted time frame. If you get to hang out in a lawn chair, it's not yours and it's not for long. Traveling means eating the whole thing because you don't have a place to refrigerate the leftovers. Traveling means living out of a suitcase that must be packed and repacked every time you wear something, wash something or buy something. There is no room for the cat. Traveling means sleeping in hotels or hostels or tents or trains or buses or the back seats of taxi cabs or nowhere at all. Traveling keeps you on your toes and on the run. It is exhausting, exhilarating and fabulous.

But it's work. It takes planning and practice to do it without killing yourself.

I leave most of the really hard stuff up to my husband, like researching, planning, booking, scheduling, paying, knowing where we are and knowing where we are going at any given time. Details. Left-brain territory. I pretty much just pack a suitcase and show up at the airport.

And even that is not as simple as it sounds. I have learned the hard way that the best traveling means that if you pack it, sometime or other during the excursion, unless you are rich, famous, notorious or pregnant, you will have to carry it.

This raises some concerns.

When you vacation by car you don't have to be careful about what you pack. You don't even have to be careful where you pack it. I have been known to throw more loose stuff in the car as an afterthought than I actually packed in my suitcase.

But when you are *traveling*, the packing process requires you to actually predict what you will need and when. For people like me, this can be more foreign than the destination itself. And, after you've addled your brains doing that, you need to fit all of your things inside of one suitcase. One! This becomes a geometric nightmare when you realize that some things will not fit in said suitcase no matter how many ways you turn or fold or crush them. Some things must be left behind. A traveler's *Sophie's Choice*.

For chronically disorganized right-brainers like me, this is torture.

And then, just when the temptation of that second suitcase seems impossible to resist, this mantra rises from the depths of the traveler's soul. "You shall bear the burden of that which you have packed. You Shall Bear the Burden of That Which You Have Packed. *YOU SHALL BEAR THE BURDEN OF THAT WHICH YOU HAVE PACKED!*"

Shaken, you back down and start again. It was in this way that I discovered the following Four Rules of Efficient Packing.

(My family is doubled over with laughter right now because I used the words "efficient" and "packing" in the same sentence. Let's ignore the naysayers and continue, shall we?)

Rule #1: Disorganized people like me must compensate for their disorganization by being ultra-organized. This goes against the grain, but it can be done. The key to organizing the disorganized is to have less stuff to organize. So, regardless of which side of your brain dictates your actions, pack light. Take what you need and only what you need. Maybe less. Fight the urge to take twelve of everything. On our recent trip to Italy, I packed seven cardigan sweaters. All colors to complement any possible wardrobe combination. I wore two of them—beige and black.

Rule #2: Unless you are hiking in the Himalayas, there will probably be stores where you are going. If you are traveling in America, you are never more than forty seconds from a Walmart, a CVS or a truck stop. Consider this when you are packing personal care items like soaps, lotions, shampoos, pantyhose, toothpaste, Dapper Dan, toothpicks, etc. You don't need to pack enough for the whole trip. At any given time, you only really need a forty-second supply of anything. If you are traveling out of the country, you may not get your favorite brands, but what's the reason for traveling if not to experience new things?

Rule #3: Choose your luggage carefully. My brother-in-law the woodworker once said, "You can do any job if you have the right tools." This goes for packing, too. The right suitcase can change your life. I was so excited when we booked our first cruise that I went out and bought a new set of luggage, one that would accommodate all the cruise wear I was sure I needed. It did. And then some. And then some more. The big case was the size of a steamer trunk and soft sided (yet rugged) so it had some g-i-v-e. I could pack my children in this suitcase if I could get them to sit still long enough. It had a zipper section on the outside that pushed out like the roof on a 1968 VW Camper Van with straps and pouches on the inside to hold all my crucial items in place. It had one-way wheels and a telescoping handle, one of the first of its kind. I struggled to pull it behind me and if I turned too fast I could take out a whole crowd of unsuspecting fellow travelers, like a big rig jackknifing on an icy highway. Empty, that sucker weighed twenty-five pounds. Packed, it tipped the airport scale at just over seventy. Remember, too, that this was just *my* bag. We were traveling as a family of four, each with his or her own leviathan in tow—plus carry-ons, the kind with shoulder straps that tipped us all 43.7 degrees to the left and twisted our spines into question marks.

In the years that it has taken me to transition from vacationer to traveler, I have realized that overpacking is like overeating. Smart dieters use small plates to make their portions look larger and more satisfying. They eat less and are happier—or so they say.

The same holds for suitcases. The more space you have, the more you'll bring because nothing is sadder than a half-packed suitcase. But on that first cruise, I only used a fraction of the fifty-plus pounds of whatever the hell it was that I brought and moving that bag anywhere was torture. Since then I have progressively downsized. For my last trip I bought a suitcase that is twenty by fifteen by eight and weighs in at just under eight pounds. It has four wheels that spin in any direction and it moves alongside me like a well-trained dog on a leash. When it was fully packed for the three-week trip, it weighed thirty-five pounds. My carry-on is now an L. L. Bean backpack that holds my stuff, fits under my seat and allows me to walk upright like other members of my species.

And you know what? I still had too much stuff. Remember the dance of the seven cardigans?

Rick Steves, travel guide-book guy extraordinaire, fits all he needs for a European trip of several weeks in his carry-on. This is my dream. I'm getting closer, but I'm not there yet. Next trip. (I said that when the last trip was the next trip. I am nothing if not a work in progress.) But, in my defense, Rick is a guy. Not to be sexist, but I doubt that I'll ever get by with two pairs of khakis, two polo shirts and a windbreaker.

So now that you've got the pack-light, go-small message, the basic question of disorganized, last-minute right-brainers remains. What should I put in the bag?

The answer? Not much.

Rule #4: Pack as I say, not as I do. I always pack too much. I once packed twelve sweaters for a three-day ski weekend. My friend asked me if I was trying to impress everyone with my sweater collection. I was surprised and hurt by this because nothing could be further from the truth. I packed twelve sweaters because I owned twelve sweaters and I didn't know which ones *not* to bring. Really. My brain lives in the moment and projecting future needs is hard for me. So, instead of agonizing over what to do, it was much easier to just take them all. It also got me to bed earlier because packing was happening, of course, in the middle of the night before. I felt vindicated later because, even though I only wore four of the sweaters over the three days (and could have gotten away with two), I told myself that I had no way of knowing which sweater I would want at any given time considering the variety of activities and the changeable snow conditions and the variability of northern New England temperatures. Luckily, I didn't have to carry that suitcase very far.

I have learned since then. It's a good thing. A recent Italian trip was three weeks of planes and trains and buses and stairs and cobblestones and more trains and more stairs and even though I was traveling the lightest that I ever have *in my life* with my nifty, featherweight, wheelie-dude suitcase and my cherry-red, ergonomically engineered L. L. Bean backpack, every day, *every day*, I wished they were lighter.

So here, finally, are some of my packing suggestions.

Before you decide anything, set aside a day to learn what you really need. Go through the whole day with a notepad and jot down every single thing you used, wore or ingested that day. Then cross everything off that you can buy where you're going, that your hotel will provide, that you can live without or that it would be stupid to carry. Chances are good that by the time you finish crossing off stuff, what you have left are prescription meds, a few personal hygiene products, an electronic communication device and the clothes on your back.

So let's start there.

- Over the counter medications are readily available anywhere, anytime in America as per the forty-second rule described earlier. But if you are traveling out of the country, you may want to consider throwing in sample sizes of basic things. I discovered the hard way that there is no such thing as Pepto Bismol in Florence. Obviously, you'll want as much room as you need for a full trip's supply of prescription meds.

- You'll want your favorite brands of deodorant, toothpaste, mouthwash, sunscreens, etc. But pay attention to how long it takes you to go through a regular-sized container. Probably a lot longer than you're going to be away. Chances are good you can make do with travel sizes or TSA approved 3-ounce bottles. If you're ever going to learn to travel with just a carry-on, you need to limit this stuff. Pack it small or buy it there. If you can, forget the hairdryer, travel iron, electric razor and Sonicare toothbrush and stick with small, manually operated items and/or things that your hotel provides. If you're not sure what they have, check their websites.

- On one trip we traveled with a laptop, an e-reader, two cameras, a cell phone and a Smartphone. Ugh! I soon realized that my Smartphone could do everything as well, if not better, than all the bigger things combined. How much weight that knowledge would have saved us! Invest in a Smartphone for everyone in your party. Totally worth it. With the space you save you can bring home some nice souvenirs.

- OK. Clothes. This is the hardest one of all. (If you are a male, you're on your own in this department. For reasons that will become obvious to you in a moment, I am directing the comments of this section to women.)

When I am tempted to pack too much, I wag my finger in my own face and recite the following:

Packing Note to Self: Unless you are being followed by the paparazzi, it really doesn't matter if you wear the same thing several times. And unless you are Kate Middleton, Lady GaGa, Miley Cyrus or Cher, no one really gives a shit what you wear ever. In other words, get over yourself. You are not famous. No one is watching you. As long as you are neat, clean and comfortable, and your suitcase is manageable and liftable, you will get along just fine. (Unless, of course, you have an entourage. In that dream you can bring all you want. Your peeps will haul the stuff and you will only have to worry about your expensive sunglasses and the bag with the yappy little dog.)

And then I get down to business.

So here, ladies, in my never-ending struggle to have what I need and carry it too, is my newly discovered packing secret. These two words will take you all around the world in style and comfort.

Ready?

Pack dresses.

I know! Brilliant, right?

Previously, I'd never pack more than one dress, if that, for a night out. Day wear would be jeans, slacks, capris and tops. Boy, do they fill up a suitcase. So this time, I tried something new and it worked like a charm. Dresses roll up beautifully for packing. They don't take up much space this way and rolling really does cut back on wrinkles. Pair them with black leggings if it's cool or if you're running for trains or taking part in other activities where the extra coverage is appreciated by everyone. You can roll them up inside a dress to save packing space and you *never* have to worry about wrinkles. Can you say that about pants? Then a lightweight cardigan or two (not seven) for evenings or cooler days and you're good! Keep colors neutral and splash it up with scarves. In Italy all women wear scarves all the time. Splurge and buy some new ones wherever you travel. If you can't travel without packing pants, toss in one pair of black pants and/or capris and a top that's appropriate to the season. But I'll bet you won't wear them. Be sure everything is machine wash and dry and plan on doing laundry at least once. On my three-week trip to Italy, I brought eight dresses. I could have gotten by with five.

To round out the wardrobe:

Two pairs of shoes. Period. Wear a pair. Pack a pair. One pair of comfortable walkers. Another pair of comfortable walkers. (Try Eastern Mountain Sports or Merrill for good walkers that don't look like sneakers or orthopedic shoes. Unless that's what you want, in which case you're on your own.) There is no discussion about this. Just do it. If you insist on three inch spike heels, buy them there, wear them out on the town, and then leave them for the maid.

Underwear. This is personal, but space is space so bring as few pieces as you can bear. The hotel room sink is your friend. Use it to rinse your undies daily. To make this easier, buy underwear for hikers (both genders) from a sporting goods shop like Dick's or Eastern Mountain Sports. It's expensive, but it fits great, washes easily and dries overnight, guaranteed. If you're really good at this, you could get by with two pairs for the whole trip. I'm not quite there yet.

Raingear. As lightweight as possible, but be sure to have something with a hood that is wind and waterproof. If it gets chilly, you can layer under it to stay dry and warm. In Europe, B & B's often have a stand full of umbrellas by the door for their guests to use but regular hotels leave you to face the elements on your own.

Miscellaneous. An extra pair of eyeglasses, a small Moleskine journal and a pen.

That's it. For my next trip, I will look at what I packed for my last trip and try to cut it back by ten pounds. This is huge for me. I can already feel the pressure. But when you're out in the world, it's amazing how little you actually need. It's lovely to travel light and the older I get the less stuff I want to lug around in general, let alone on a trip. I long for the day when I can fly away confidently, my necessary possessions contained in one small bag stored in the compartment above my head. I don't know if I'll ever be brave or seasoned enough to accomplish that, but I'll keep trying.

Meanwhile, in the absence of an entourage, I will continue to bear the burden of that which I have packed, whatever form it may take.

Because, when you come right down to it, what other choice is there?

Saving *Your* Life

- Are you a good traveler? How so (or not)?

- Open up your imaginary perfect suitcase. What would it look like? What would it contain?

- Have you ever come home from a trip being able to say that you used everything you packed? Describe the trip.

- What were your worst packing mistakes?

- If you are disorganized, what steps do you take to compensate and get things done?

- If you carry a purse or a back pack or a book bag in your daily travels, what's in it? Do you need it all every day? If not, why do you carry it all around with you?

- Have you ever been on a trip when you could not find something you absolutely needed? How did you get along without it? If you were OK, did you really need it?

- Think about your packing habits. What must you have with you when you travel? What have you learned to travel without? What does this say about you?

- How do your packing skills (or lack of them) reflect your strengths and weaknesses in life?

- What we want is often very different from what we need. If you were to cut your living space by half, what could you do without?

- Did anything else about this essay remind you of your own experiences? In your notebook, jot down one memory, thought or opinion that popped into your head as you were reading.

Part Five
Spring Forward, Fall Back

You can't be a New Englander unless you have defined your relationship with winter. In southern New England, our winters run the gamut from mild extensions of autumn to blustery, blizzardy, bleak affairs that transform our homes into igloos, ice palaces or icicle prisons.

Whatever form a winter takes, I'm good with it for a while. It's fun to stoke up the fireplace, bake brownies and pull out the homemade afghans, woolly sweaters, fuzzy slippers and thick books. No other time of year gives you permission to put life on hold for a while and just get cozy. When four feet of snow gets dumped on your doorstep, there's not much else you can do.

It's the only time of year that I drink tea.

I'm fine with winter through the holidays. By January, though, I start to feel antsy and by February, I'm done. I'm tired of being cold. Of clearing snow. Of watching my step. Of keeping track of the hats and scarves and gloves that I'm always losing. Of having fun stuff cancelled.

And soon after that, full-blown cabin fever sets in and all I want is spring.

But if you think that a New England spring brings respite

after the cold, harsh winter, you've got another thing coming. Spring here is nothing but a tease. Give a little. Take a lot. One step forward. Two steps back. Those who trust the calendar and jump too quickly into spring often live to regret it.

The vernal equinox means nothing here—it's just another cold day. If you're smart, you know the whereabouts of your driving gloves until at least April. You never plant your marigolds before Memorial Day Weekend for fear of a rogue frost. And you keep the kettle on the back burner until you're really, really sure that tea season has passed.

You can see that I have strong feelings about this. I guess that's why I keep writing about it. And, unless spring starts playing nice with us, I don't see myself stopping anytime soon.

The essays in this section are me giving spring a piece of my mind.

Winter's Last Hurrah or
We Dare the Ides of March

Friday, February 28

Winter in New England is a long, tempestuous affair and by now even those who love it are getting weary of its demands. Turning the calendar page to March brings a moment of unexplainable relief to New Englanders, one that mitigates what we see and feel as we step outside.

Forecasters are predicting a big snowstorm for Monday. That means another round of cancellations, another confrontation with snow blowers and plows and another batch of chicken chili. Dressing to go out will require time and layers and help to insure that everything is tucked and covered. Driving will be slippery and we will worry until the last of the family has skidded back into the driveway and is sitting safely in front of the TV, wrapped in an afghan and slurping from a bowl of warm chili.

But today the sun is out, the roads are clear and the air is still. It's nearly noon and, after an early morning wind chill advisory, the sun has warmed us up to a balmy seventeen degrees. That means we have plenty of time to make the storm preparations that we could do in our sleep. Groceries enough for a few days? Check. Cat food? Check. Bird seed (aka squirrel food)? Check. Batteries for flashlights and propane for the gas grill in case of power outages? Check and check. Gasoline for the snow blower? Check. Full gas tanks in the cars? Check. Electronics charged and ready? Check-a-roni.

Bring it on.

We face it with confidence, but we are tired of it.

We will get through it by grasping onto any little shred of evidence that spring is in the wings.

Seeing March atop the calendar page is a biggie. We know from past experience that no matter how bad things get in March, and they can get pretty bad, it is still March. March is not January. A big storm in January is just the beginning of a long season of cold, dark isolation. Of hunkering down for the long haul. Of setting up the jigsaw puzzle table in the dining room. Of caching in enough yarn to crochet yet another afghan. Of making a list of the indoor house projects that need to get done but probably won't. Of rereading *Ethan Frome*. Of wishing we could hibernate and wake up with the bears in April.

But a big storm in March is a different story. We are less accepting, less resigned to the inevitability of it all. We are angrier and more aggressive. Every March storm could very well be the last of the season. We shake our fists and meet them head-on because now they seem defeatable. Even if a lot of snow falls, its days are numbered. It won't be long now, we can say as we look at the calendar. We've got this. We own you.

We can never say that in January.

There are other clues that winter is gasping its last. They may be hard to see but they are all around us. We know because we are looking so damned hard for them.

And at this point, we'll take anything, really.

So, even before the snow disappears from the roof, before the buds bud, before the grass makes its first tentative appearance and before the temperatures stay above freezing for more than a couple of days at a time, I have found the following reasons to believe that it's almost spring in New England.

- The sun doesn't set until 5:30.
- I'm losing the inclination to go to bed right after supper.
- Our street is once again wide enough for two cars to pass.
- Neighbors whose mailboxes were casualties of the snow plows can't rely on the snow banks to hold them up anymore.
- Kids and teachers, both cheering the snow in December, groan at the thought of another snow day.
- Our southern relatives have started posting Facebook pictures of themselves in short-sleeved shirts, tending their gardens and riding their bicycles. We say we are happy for them. But we're not.
- I hate my coat.
- Old people are trickling back from Florida. I know because they push their carts around the Stop & Shop looking fit and tanned and not winter-weary at all. They buy jelly donuts and kale.
- *Downton Abbey* has come—and gone. If only winter were as short as their season!
- My friend Mikey C. gets all worked up over the Red Sox Truck Day. I don't know what it is either, but it's only once a year and he's a nice guy so we humor him.

- Baseball stories are finding their way into the evening news. And Facebook posts. And dinner conversations. Fantasy League owners are polishing up their picks.

- Basketball stories are finding their way into the evening news. And Facebook posts. And dinner conversation. Office pool commissioners are polishing up their brackets.

- The *Lands' End* bathing suit catalog has arrived and is sitting on the coffee table.

- I notice that my jeans are a little tight and I get on the scale for the first time since Christmas. This annual moment of self-loathing happens because the *Lands' End* bathing suit catalog has arrived and is sitting on the coffee table.

- I dust off the treadmill, hoping that the weather will get warm enough for me to walk outside before I have no other choice but to use it.

- The sweaters and outerwear that have taken up so much space on clearance racks in local department stores are slowly being replaced by pretty pastel things.

- The squirrels have completely hijacked the bird feeder and I have let them.

- The few stupid robins that have been here all winter are being joined by their smarter cousins who seem surprised that it is still so cold.

- Our cat woke up today. Twice.

- A letter came from the tree guy about treating our snow tree. It's really a crab apple, but when it blossoms it looks exactly the same as it does when the wet, sticky snow clings to its branches. In the winter it reminds us of spring. In the spring it reminds us of winter. But in a good way.

- Signs have sprung up out of the snow on little wires all around town reminding parents to sign their kids up for a vast assortment of spring sports. Do we have enough kids in town for all these sports?

- The tops of the solar walkway lights that I forgot to take in last fall have nearly resurfaced from under the snow. Last night they gave off an eerie, muted glow under a thin layer of ice—like Poe characters released from their premature burials. Yikes.

- The Ziploc bag of baby carrots that I apparently dropped on my way to the car two months ago has reappeared on the edge of the driveway.

- We wonder what else we're going to find under the snow when it all melts.

- My former favorite hoody is getting on my nerves.

- We start to feel an urge to ice that tea. And fill it with sugar. And take it outside. On a patio. By a pool. We know that this dream is still months away.

- Leprechauns and shamrocks have replaced Christmas wreaths and Valentine hearts on people's front doors.

- Cadbury Eggs have returned to CVS.

- If I am on my back porch facing south between 12:04 p.m. and 12:27 p.m. on a sunny day, and I stand directly in a sunbeam and click my heels together three times, I can feel the sun generating warmth on my face. Sort of.

- I now believe that losing an hour of sleep is a small price to pay for an extra hour of daylight. Give me some Daylight Savings Time!
- I make lists like this to remind myself that the seasons, they do indeed go round. When winter comes, can spring be far behind?

Well, yes. Yes it can. But when March comes, it's a different story. Look out, Frosty. Even your magic hat can't save you now.

Monday, March 3

The predicted storm that sent everyone to the grocery store over the weekend went, ironically, to our south. It snowed somewhere, but not here. We've had a string of sunny, frigid days, and, after overnight lows in the single digits, today's high temps will cap out at a chilly twenty-six degrees. School is in session, the snow blower is in the garage and I haven't seen a plow in days. Old Man Winter is losing his clout. Right now, local meteorologists are giving him about two weeks to live. Their optimism amuses me. I'd give him longer than that. All we really know is that he's here today, giving us all he's got left. He's a stubborn old geezer and we know that he'll fight till the very end. As well he should.

As should we all.

Saving *Your* Life

- Lists are fantastic! They organize us and they help us to generate ideas. In your journal, make a list of things that you would like to make lists about. Then, start one. And another. And maybe another! They're addictive! I guarantee that you will have a page full of writing ideas in no time. Any given item on any given list opens a door to you and is worth saving.

- Choose one list and write about its significance.

- Choose *one* item from *one* list and tell its story.

- When we personify winter, we give him feelings and a point of view. How will he feel about being beaten down and replaced? How would you feel in his place?

- List all of your favorite things about your favorite season.

- Look out your window and imagine what it looks like in another season. Can you?

- How do you make it through a long, cold winter?

- Does your diet change with the seasons? What are some of your favorite winter recipes?

- Describe some of your favorite seasonal outdoor activities.

- Did anything else about this essay remind you of your own experiences? In your notebook, jot down one memory, thought or opinion that popped into your head as you were reading.

The Rights of Spring

It is April 30, 2014. We are over a month into a New England spring. It is raining steadily and is as bleak a day as we would expect to see in November. The current temperature is forty-three degrees and it is not expected to go any higher than fifty today. There will be no sun. We have had a few warm spring days, a very few, and we can't seem to string together more than two or three sunny days in a row. Even then, we're thrilled with a temperature anywhere near sixty. Anything warmer seems ethereal and far away. Trees that have blossomed by now in years passed are struggling to bud. Birds seem dumbfounded by this turn of events and the daffodils that were brave enough to blossom are shivering in their beds. Pedestrians slosh through puddles with their collars turned up and hats pulled down. We're cold, damn it. And wet. And not feeling springy at all.

We would have tolerated this a month ago. March is notoriously fickle. But we expect some tenderness from April, especially the end of April—a kind hand extended to help us squint our way back in to the sunlight and out of the clutches of winter. But that's not what we got.

Spring this year seems to have an attitude problem.

So who can we accuse when we are the victims of a season's underperformance and lack of motivation? Where is the first place we look when standards of any sort are not being met? Where do we turn when we need scapegoats who will not only accept responsibility but will work to fix things—even things that are totally out of their realm?

I know!

When in doubt, blame a teacher.

*****

Meanwhile, in the cyberspace of the local public high school, the following email exchange may very well be taking place.

Dear Parents of Spring,

This is to inform you that your child is not working up to her potential. We would like to schedule a meeting with you to discuss her recent disappointing performance in the areas of temperature raising, blossom cultivation and mood elevation. We believe she is capable. We need to explore her reasons for refusing to put these basic skills into practice this year. Her attitude is having an adverse effect on all of us and we hope that you can help us to motivate her.

Please call at your earliest convenience. We'd like to get to the bottom of this before summer vacation.

Sincerely,

Spring's Teachers

Dear Spring's Teachers,

This is to inform *you* that I, too, am distressed by my little girl's performance, but it's not her fault. Our family situation has been strained because Spring's grandfather, Old Man Winter has moved in with us and made himself comfortable—so comfortable that we can't get rid of him. We only took him in because we thought he would be dead by now.

This situation has had other unexpected consequences. Spring's father, Summer, has gone south, leaving us to fend for ourselves. Money has become an issue and poor Spring has found it impossible to afford the new fashions of the season and has been forced to stretch her wardrobe by continuing to wear the coats and sweaters that were all the rage in February. So, she only lets things warm up as much as her wardrobe will allow. Then she lets the temperatures plunge again until she has saved enough money to buy herself another cute outfit. She can only afford to go the mall once a week these days. You can understand the emotional effect this can have on a young girl.

She is doing the best that she can under the circumstances and I think that your impatience with her is just making things worse. She texted me from English class today saying that she was being forced to endure a reading of Shelley's "Ode to the West Wind." She held it together until the line, "If Winter comes, can Spring be far behind?" I can't believe that she is being subjected to such insensitivity. I texted her back and told her to go to the clinic and lie down. She said she would stick it out because class was almost over and she didn't want to risk being late to lunch on taco day. She is such a little trooper.

So, if you could just be patient with her, she'll get around to her work when she's ready.

Sincerely,

Spring's Mom

Dear Spring's Mom,

We are very sorry to hear about Spring's difficulties. But we are coming up on the end of the term and Spring has not made any attempt to complete her late work. We are freezing here. Her average temperature this week has been a disappointing forty-five. But, since school policy no longer allows failing temperatures, we will enter her average in as a sixty and overlook the rain. She will, of course, pass the term regardless of her performance, but we think, for the good of humanity, that she could be doing better. Her guidance counselor will be speaking to her to discuss her progress and see if there is anything else we can do on our end to help motivate her to be the best that she can be. Perhaps we will take her shopping.

School administration has made it clear to us that this is a result of our poor performance and not Spring's, so we will redouble our efforts to rectify the problem without putting Spring's scholarship opportunities at risk.

Sincerely,

Spring's Teachers

Dear Spring's Teachers,

The shopping trip sounds like a great idea. If she had a few more cute outfits, she would be more willing to warm things up to a seasonally appropriate level. And, since no scholarship committee will look at that sixty, I think bumping her average up to an eighty will motivate her to perform better. Then, when it comes time for us to fill out the parent portion of the new teacher evaluation document, I could put a good word in for you with the other mothers in my book club. Right now, things are not looking so good for you.

Sincerely,

Spring's Mom

Dear Spring's Mom,

Thank you so much for your support of our efforts to educate your child and keep our jobs. After much discussion, it has been decided that Spring will never receive anything lower than a B on her report cards regardless of whether or not the work has been completed. She will be allowed to do anything in school that keeps her happy, including texting in class and leaving early for the cafeteria on taco day. And, she will be transported regularly by school bus to the mall where each week one of her teachers will treat her to a really cute outfit.

All we ask in return is that she score well on her standardized tests and that she warm us up a little. New England is depending on her. We are cold here. And wet. And not very springy at all.

No pressure, you understand.

Sincerely,

Spring's Teachers

Dear Spring's Teachers,

I don't appreciate the tone of your last correspondence. The stress you have placed on my daughter to perform has frozen her in her tracks. She is crying in her room right now because she had to stay home from the mall in order to work on your ridiculous demands. The rubric that you sent home outlining your expectations is unreasonable even with all but two requirements crossed out. You must understand that we raised Spring to have a mind of her own and we will not stand by and let you shape it any way you want to. She is smart and capable, but she will not perform according to your whims. She will not make the flowers bloom just to make you look good.

Now, you will need to do better if you are to get Spring to appear. Two weekly trips to the mall at your expense and no deadlines might just coax Spring out of her shell and satisfy the ladies of my book club.

And my lawyer.

Sincerely,

Spring's Mom

Dear Spring's Mom,

We give up. We will do anything you ask. We are at your mercy. We will extend the grading period indefinitely and allow Spring free reign in class and out. She can do the assignments that she likes and forget the rest. She will be graded on effort instead of quality unless she doesn't choose to expend any effort in which case she will be graded on whatever cute outfit she is wearing that day. She will always pass with at least a B and she will never be reprimanded for missing due dates or texting in class. We will smile in her presence. We will stand when she enters a room and curtsy when she leaves. We will take her to the mall every day. We will do our best to tailor our programs here to Spring's every need. Just please don't hurt us.

Sincerely,

Spring's Teachers

Dear Spring's Teachers,

Deal. I'll have my lawyer draw up the papers for your signature.

Sincerely,

Spring's Mom

Dear Tiffany,

You won't believe the cute outfit that my teacher just bought me at the mall! It might be worth cranking up the temp a few degrees so that I can wear it to school tomorrow! Tell the birds and flowers to get ready! I'll text you from class to let you know what time I'll be leaving for lunch! I'm free because my English teacher is writing my college essay and my guidance counselor is filling out all of my college applications for me! And guess what??? Daddy is coming home and Grandpa is almost dead!!!!! I feel so much better! All I have to do now is throw down a couple of seventy degree days, and everyone starts drooling over me!!!! Looks like I'll be graduating with honors!!!!! I didn't know it could be this easy!!!!!!!!!!!!!!!!!!!!!

Now if I could just get my mom to buy me a car! She's such a bitch sometimes! Maybe I can get my guidance counselor to call her and tell her that I'd be so much happier if I had a car!

I love my life!!!!!!!!!!!!!!!!!!!!!

Luv ya,

Spring

*****

It is May 1, 2014. After a night of cold temperatures and torrential downpours, the ground is saturated and the sky is gray.

But, it's not raining anymore and the temperatures are creeping up. The weather report promises that the current temperature of fifty-three will rise to seventy degrees late this afternoon and will stay there for an hour or two—just in time for people to enjoy a walk after work. The promise for the week ahead includes highs in the mid to upper sixties with a mix of sun and clouds—mostly sun.

It's late, that's for sure. But relief seems to be in sight.

A little bit of sunshine goes a long way.

Looks like those teachers are finally doing their jobs.

Saving *Your* Life

- Make a list of things that bother you. Choose one and find someone to blame for it.

- Write about a time when someone else's laziness made your life harder—or vice versa.

- This essay personifies Spring, Summer and Winter. Choose a season, give it human qualities and write a conversation you might have with it.

- How's the weather in your neck of the woods? How is the transition from winter to spring going for you?

- Teachers are perfect scapegoats. Write about a time when you were able to blame a teacher for your own shortcomings.

- Now that you know better, write a letter of apology to that teacher.

- Write about a time when you played adults against each other to get something you wanted.

- Write about a teacher who helped you more than you realized at the time.

- Write that teacher a thank-you letter.

- Did anything else about this essay remind you of your own experiences? In your notebook, jot down one memory, thought or opinion that popped into your head as you were reading.

Oh, My Achin' April

Spring shows up in New England whenever it damned well feels like it. And even though we wait for it by the window for weeks, when it gets here, we are never ready.

Oh we say we are. We are so tired of snow and cold that we whimper our way through March, cursing our coats and complaining about our southern Facebook friends who are already posting pictures of tulips and daffodils and azaleas the size of Easter lilies. We fondle our windbreakers and light sweaters and dream of the day when we can stash our scarves and gloves and hats in the appropriate Rubbermaid tub in the basement. "Good riddance," we will say. But not yet. We've learned to wait.

We've been conned by spring before.

By April Fool's Day impulsive middle-schoolers, still unschooled in the realities of life, toss their outerwear in the bushes by the bus stop and swear through the goosebumps that they're not cold at all. They look pasty and pathetic, shivering on the corner outside my house. They may have outgrown Santa Claus and the Easter Bunny, but they still believe that they can trust the calendar, poor things. Their youth and the long winter have conspired against them.

But we old timers know that it's not time yet. Soon, we hope, but we can't be certain. The only thing we know for sure is this:

April is a bitch.

And the morsel of spring that she deigns to toss us follows no discernible patterns and makes no lasting promises.

So, to avoid looking like dummies at the bus stop, we take our emergence slow.

*****

You'd never know that we were the same people who went kicking and screaming into winter just a few months ago. We go through this charade every year. Then, when we can't fight it anymore, we hunker down for the duration. This usually happens after the holidays when all the winter wonderland bullshit wears off and we can stop pretending that we are in control. We sing songs like "Let It Snow, Let It Snow, Let It Snow" because, really, what choice do we have? Resignation sets in and we suit up, we stock up, we shore up and we shut down.

In retirement, I have become a world-class hunkerer. And this past winter's eight-week, four-foot snow pack with drifts to the eaves and temperatures in the freezer gave me the perfect excuse to spend days and days in front of the fireplace, reading, writing, crocheting, learning Italian, sorting recipes and, well, hunkering. I've discovered that I'm quite good at it and had no problem not leaving the house for days at a time. A January visit to a warm, snow-free North Carolina was a pleasant diversion, but returning home to snuggle up by the fire with a couple of homemade afghans and a cat was kind of nice, too.

A bad winter gives those of us who can stay indoors an excuse to become unconscionably lazy. This year, once the cold settled in, my daily neighborhood walking regimen went to hell, even with a treadmill in the house. The free weights, untouched since Thanksgiving, have each molded their own distinguishable indentations into the carpet. And with New England springs that take their sweet-ass time and Aprils that give us no assurance of anything accept anticipation, it's tough to break out of that afghan cocoon that I've crocheted for myself and face the world again.

*****

At the end of March, I spent a week visiting my daughter in South Carolina. Temperatures danced from the sixties to the eighties. The spring flowers, except for a few stubborn tulips, had already blossomed and passed. The azaleas were in full bloom and drifting pollen left a dusty coating on anything that didn't move. I stowed my coat in the car, shaved my legs up far enough to wear capris, shook the wrinkles out of my light sweater, broke open a fresh bottle of sunscreen and strolled out amongst palm trees and little green lizards and ancient live oaks and foggy Spanish moss that swayed so fashionably in the gentle southern breeze. It was spring here. Full blown. Beautiful. Like a dream. And it was still March. April here would be dependable, predictable, gracious. Not the New England imp of a month that would be waiting for me when I got back home—bless its heart.

And, wonderful as it all was, I wasn't ready. While I enjoyed the beaches and the flowers and the warmth of the sun, I knew that throwing a couple of pairs of capris and a pink cardigan sweater into a suitcase doth not an adequate transition to spring make. There was snow on the ground when I left home. The temperature was forty degrees on a warm day and could dip back into the thirties without warning. My bed socks were still folded neatly alongside my nightstand, probably still warm from the last time I wore them. I was out of shape and out of touch from being housebound and liking it. I had a lot of catching up to do.

*****

And now that I am home and it is April, the transition has begun in earnest. I will no longer ignore the fact that the jeans that fit perfectly last October are now noticeably snug and that I need to pull the bathroom scale out from the closet and the weights up from their indents in the floor. The snow has melted to reveal a yard in dire need of attention--soggy, brown, covered in twigs and branches from the harsh winter and strewn with dead leaves left over from the distant autumn. The flower beds are bare, the window boxes are full of nut husks left behind by arrogant squirrels and the trees look like bouquets of sticks, suspended willy-nilly from the sky. The usually early-blooming forsythia bushes still show no signs of buds—late, even by our standards. There is a lot of work to be done by all of us before we New Englanders can say that spring is here.

It is overwhelming. Because, here, it is winter until it's not. We can't get down to the business of spring until we are sure that winter has left the building. March lies to our faces when it hands us a sham of an equinox with no sign of warmth. And April is just a tease. She dotes on other parts of the country and allows them to enjoy her, but, for some reason, she prefers to antagonize us, as if somewhere along the line the Northeast offended her enough to be the victims of her capricious revenge forever after.

She wags her azaleas and cherry blossoms under our noses like candy and then makes us go to the back of the line. She raises the temperatures just enough to make us put away our coats and snow shovels and then plunges us back into a deep freeze for the fun of it, like Lucy making promises to Charlie Brown right before yanking away the football.

We have learned not to trust her. We are weary of winter, but wary of spring. It's exhausting.

*****

So we wait until we know it's over or until we are reasonably sure that the earth has turned us too far toward the sun to let snooty little April have her way with us anymore. And then we poke our noses outside and see what needs to be done.

And it's a lot.

And we know that the season here is short and there is no time to waste. We've got to get to it. Now. And so we plunge in. All at once.

We open the windows as wide as we can. We dust and vacuum and polish and scrub and clean out the winter from ceilings to baseboards. We throw away and pack away and give away and rearrange. We rake and we trim and we plant and we fertilize and we mow and we bundle and we haul and we spruce. We scrape and we paint and we reattach. We walk and we bike and we skate and we fish and we jog and we chat with neighbors we haven't seen face-to-face in months. We tick chores off of our to-do list, update it for tomorrow, throw back a couple of Advil and fall into bed, bruised, sore, exhausted, invigorated, rejuvenated, hopeful.

April in New England will kill you if you let her. She's a scheming, manipulative little vixen. But when she's gone, so is winter—for real. And we are finally in the clear.

Come what May.

Saving *Your* Life

- What chores does spring have in store for you this year? Are you ready for them?

- How do you keep in shape over the winter? Do you maintain an exercise regimen even when you can't get outdoors?

- If you, like me, live in the Northeast, do you love the winter? If not, how do you escape it?

- Many native New Englanders eventually move south for good. Will you? Why or why not?

- How would you feel about year-round spring and summer?

- Do you do your own yard work? Gardening, lawn care, cleaning up after a hard winter? How do you feel about that?

- Are you inclined to jump into projects without adequate preparation? Tell about a specific project you may have taken on before you were ready.

- How easily do you make the transition from winter clothes that cover everything to spring clothes that expose more of you than the world has seen in a while? What's been going on under those clothes all winter? Is your body ready to be seen or is there some work to be done?

- Did anything else about this essay remind you of your own experiences? In your notebook, jot down one memory, thought or opinion that popped into your head as you were reading.

Part Six
Life's Lessons

No matter how much we know about life, it's never enough.

People who think they know everything there is to know have been grievously misinformed.

There is always something else, something new, something frightening, something wonderful. We spend all of our lives learning how to live. When we stop, we die.

So, we look forward and we look back. When we see the past in relation to the present, the past looks different and the present makes more sense. If we are truthful, we learn to see ourselves not as significant, autonomous entities but as pieces of a puzzle. Small, interdependent pieces.

Even so, we may reach a point when we believe that we have existed long enough to stop searching. We've got all we need. Maybe we could just *live* now.

And, then, just as we think we have a handle on things, we see that the sands beneath us are ever-shifting, making the familiar unfamiliar and the old new, making our standards obsolete and our understanding tenuous.

There is so much that we don't know—that we'll never know. We live and learn to live as best we can.

The essays in this section deal with some of the lessons that life offers to us as we live it. Learning to admit and accept our limitations, to acknowledge the past and its contributions to the present, to adjust to the changes wrought by time and youth and new ideas, to recognize and align our lives with the cycles of the natural world, to die with dignity—all worthy lessons that can enrich our lives. But, the most important lesson these essays have taught me is this—the best way to come to terms with who you are and what you know and how you live is to write about it. For me, *that* is the lesson of a lifetime.

The Girl Who Sang

I sing a little.

When I was in the fourth grade, something prompted me to approach my music teacher and ask if I could sing a solo in the spring concert. I have no idea what made me think I could do this.

My only previous performing experience was singing along to the hits of the day while tuned in to WPOP at 1410 on the AM dial. At first I crooned along with Bobby Darin and Lesley Gore and the Everly Brothers in the back seat of my sister's car when my mother made her take me to the beach with her grown-up, teen-aged friends, but once February, 1964, came and changed the face of pop music forever, I abandoned my sister's music for good.

I had found my own.

My musical world was filled with The Beatles, The Rolling Stones, Gerry and the Pacemakers, The Dave Clark Five, The Temptations, Freddie and the Dreamers, Herman's Hermits, Paul Revere and the Raiders, The Young Rascals, The Supremes, Sonny and Cher, The Miracles, Petula Clark, The Lovin' Spoonful, Bobby Sherman and a million others—the stuff of *16 Magazine*, Lloyd Thaxton's *Tiger Beat*, TV's *Shindig!*, *Hullabaloo, The Ed Sullivan Show* and, of course, AM radio. I retreated to my room each night after dinner to listen to the radio and to devour the magazines that were strewn across the floor. I cut the yummiest pictures out and squirreled them away in a box under my bed with plans for a giant, full-wall collage that I would somehow talk my mother into letting me staple into the wall paper. I knew what my faves ate for breakfast, what their favorite colors were, where they grew up, what they liked to do in their spare time, where they were performing next, what they thought of New York and how much they loved performing for their adoring fans.

And I knew their songs.

I sang them incessantly. They weren't hard to learn and I loved to sing along. I had a little transistor AM radio that took a nine-volt battery and had an earphone for privacy. Primitive by today's standards, but it was my ticket to a musical world all my own.

So I must have figured that I could sing. But again, I don't know what made me so bold as to actually approach the teacher to ask for a solo. We were not a family of singers. There were no church choirs or pickin' out tunes around a campfire or holiday sing-a-longs around the piano. In fact, there was no piano and no push to pursue music instruction outside of school. No one who was within earshot of my caterwauling with the radio ever complimented my technique or encouraged me to continue. Mostly what I heard was, "Turn that damned thing off and go to bed."

I guess I figured that, if you love something enough, you must be good at it. So I took a shot.

My fourth grade music teacher was Miss Kyle. She was a reed

in the breeze, so slim as to almost disappear if you weren't paying attention. Since the popular culture of the day thought nothing of pinching my cheeks and calling me "Chubby," I noticed such things, even then. She wore flowered dresses and had mousy brown hair and glasses that scootched down her nose. When she conducted the fourth grade chorus in our Mary Poppins medley, she threw her whole body into it and sometimes I thought the magical force of our singing might lift her right off her feet and that we should be careful.

I don't remember what Miss Kyle said to me when I approached her with such boldness. But I do remember what she didn't say.

She didn't say no.

And so, at the concert that spring, after stepping down from the risers that held the fourth grade chorus and handing off my cardboard and cellophane Mary Poppins hat with the big paper flower made with love by the Mothers' Club, I made my solo singing debut. I was the featured soloist in a little musical skit with Howard, a boy from the third grade who played my little brother. As he sat down on the edge of the stage, dressed like Huckleberry Finn with a fishing pole, a straw hat, raggedy pants and bare feet, I admonished him for his hooky-playing ways while Miss Kyle sat down at the piano and played the introductory measures of my song. Then I segued seamlessly into the opening chorus of "Swingin' on a Star." I wore a white dress with blue smocking, white anklets and black patent-leather shoes, what all the fashionable fourth-grade divas were wearing that year, and I sashayed across the stage wagging my finger at this wayward boy, working my way through the mule verse, the pig verse and the fish verse. With each one he became increasingly remorseful and, when I reached the climactic monkey verse, the young truant, miraculously reformed, leapt to his feet and sang along. Big finish! Applause! Thunderous! Life-altering! Ice cream sundaes all around!

From that moment on, I was the girl who sang. The go-to girl. If there was a song that needed singing at my elementary school, I was the one who sang it. So while I was rocking to the radio by night, I was singing show tunes by day—among them "Who Will Buy?" from *Oliver*, "Beautiful Candy" from *Carnival*, the fifth grade spring concert featured solo "You'll Never Walk Alone" from *Carousel* and my sixth grade spring concert triumph, "The Impossible Dream" from *The Man of LaMancha*. I was never nervous then. I learned my lyrics just like I learned the words to songs on the radio that I remember to this day and took each performance in stride. I accepted my applause with a curtsy and went instantly back to being a kid, arguing with my mother and struggling to get up for school in the morning. I loved singing, but I never felt like it was a big deal. It was just a thing I did. When I was finished, life was exactly the same as it had been before. The things that I felt weird about didn't go away. But the music gave me something to not feel weird about and that was enough. And I never had to ask again. They asked me. The songs on the radio were not the songs that they asked me to sing in school. But I knew now why the singers kept on singing them. I kept the radio on as much as I could.

My reputation followed me, but things changed. I still sang in junior high and high school. But I was no longer *the* girl who sang. I was *a* girl who sang. I wasn't the go-to girl when there was a song to be sung. I was one of several. In the presence of other strong singers my childhood boldness was replaced by self-consciousness and doubt. I sang in all the school groups I could find and if the director noticed me and asked me to sing something special I would happily comply. But I would never ask. There were other featured solos but they didn't automatically go to me. The most memorable was when our high school music director asked me to sing the part of Amahl's mother in a senior-year Christmas performance of Gian Carlo Menotti's *Amahl and the Night Visitors*. Now *that* was a night. Challenging and glorious. Sometimes its passages still pop into my head.

It was followed by *not* getting cast as a lead by the same director in the spring production of *South Pacific*, a musical I have detested ever since. Now, I am grateful for having had the opportunity to sing in such a wonderful production as the Menotti. But back then I would have traded Mrs. Amahl for Nellie Forbush or Bloody Mary in a heartbeat. The message to me was that I was good, but not that good. Not the go-to. If I wanted it, I'd have to work for it. Compete. Improve. Put myself out there. Learn to be tough in the face of rejection. Not give up.

Losing the part I expected should have made me hungrier. It should have taught me a lesson in how to navigate the realities of life. How to brush myself off and get back in the game. Real artists learn to balance rejection with success and concentrate on their love of what they do. They know what I knew intrinsically in the fourth grade, that if you love something you just walk up to the teacher one day and ask for it. The chips will fall where they fall. Not trying is the worst failure of all.

But all of that takes confidence. Somewhere between the fourth grade and the twelfth, mine diminished. Losing that part did not make me stronger. Instead it broke my spirit and I didn't do the show at all. Nor any since.

And whose fault is that?

My musical career, as it turns out, peaked in the sixth grade.

I never studied music formally after graduating high school. Never trained my voice or mastered an instrument. Fear of failure, I think, kept me from pursuing it, even though my high school director made it clear to me that I was the only one in our school who could have sung the Menotti and that he chose to do it mostly because of me. Why did I let the failure trump the success?

I'll never know.

I grew up and moved on. I studied literature, became an English teacher, married, raised a family and filled my life with other wonderful things. There have been lots of successes—lots to be proud of.

But music loitered stubbornly on the outskirts of my life and wouldn't leave me alone.

It nagged to get in, like a cat yowling at the back door. I told myself that there was no time or money for me to pursue it properly. I attended lots of concerts and plays, saw to it that my kids got lessons in piano and band instruments, read audition notices in the paper, sang informally with friends, even went back to church mostly because I enjoyed singing the liturgy and familiar hymns. And that, for a long time, was enough.

And then it wasn't.

I discovered then that you don't have to be a diva to be a

singer. I discovered that you don't have to be a soloist to feel the joy of great music. I discovered that if you want to be a singer, all you have to do is to find someplace to sing.

There are more opportunities than you might imagine, if only you put yourself out there.

I sing now in local choruses that perform great works—Mozart, Duruflé, Verdi, Handel, Brahms, Bach, stuff I thought I could never learn. Our concerts are acclaimed and well-attended. I once sang the Duruflé Requiem with a choir at Lincoln Center. And, I sang the Verdi Requiem in a choir directed by John Rutter at Carnegie Hall. Featured soloist? Not even close. Second soprano, seventh row, fifth from the right. But I was there. In the room. On the stage. Singing my heart out and feeling the joy.

So, you see, as "Swingin' on a Star" tried to teach me in the fourth grade, it was all up to me. I should have listened.

On the way out of the auditorium on the night of my fourth grade debut, my mother was accosted by a neighbor, annoyed that we had been keeping my singing lessons a secret. She had been surprised by my performance and believed, for some reason, that she had a right to know. My mother took great joy in telling that nosy neighbor that I never had a singing lesson in my life. I had natural talent.

Maybe so. But I had a lot to learn.

Saving *Your* Life

- What part does music play in your life? Surely it's in there somewhere. Make a list of memorable musical experiences that have affected you somehow. Then choose one and elaborate on the event.

- Look back on a time when you did something as a kid that surprises you now. Where did you get the boldness? When did you lose it? Did you lose it?

- Think of a time when your parents were most proud of you. How did you know? How did you feel?

- Make a list of things that you liked or did well as a kid that you stopped doing as you grew up. How many things on that list would you like to take up again? Choose one item on the list and plan a comeback.

- Popular music often defines us as members of a certain generation. Make a list of songs that you remember from your formative years.

- How many of those lyrics are still in your head?

- How do you react to rejection? Think of a time when you didn't win. Write about what you did as a result.

- What comes easily to you? How has this talent played a part in your life? Have you worked to develop it? Should you have?

- Did anything else about this essay remind you of your own experiences? In your notebook, jot down one memory, thought or opinion that popped into your head as you were reading.

Maycomb, McKinley Drive and Me

One and done.

That's how I feel about lots of books and movies I've encountered. One go-around was enough. In some of the more unfortunate cases, once was more than enough. Sometimes way more.

But every great once in a while a book comes along that defines a way of life so completely and so honestly that reentering its world is like visiting an old friend—something you look forward to and want to do as often as you can. And if you're lucky, someone takes that very book and makes it into one of the most beloved movies of all time. Harper Lee's *To Kill a Mockingbird* is one of those books.

After teaching the book to tenth graders for thirty years, you'd think I'd be done with it. It's true that there are whole chapters that come back to me after reading the first paragraph and pages of dialog that I can recite in my sleep. I can hum the background music from the film in all the right places and perform accurately along with the actors in all of my favorite scenes and then some—right down to Scout's accent and Atticus's dramatic pauses.

So what's the attachment?

It's pretty simple.

I admire the book and still get emotionally involved in the movie, not only because of the story's social message, but also because of how much it reminds me of my own childhood. Even though Scout and Jem Finch are growing up in the Deep South in the mid-1930s and I grew up in New England in the early 1960s, we lived in very much the same world. Eight-year-olds in 1963 didn't know that we were sitting on a powder keg and that the world around us was about to explode any more than Scout understood how Atticus was blowing the lid off of things in Maycomb in 1935, ironically for many of the same reasons. We were just kids, imitating our parents, tolerating school, and longing for summer. Like Scout, we reveled in our innocence and thought that what we were living was real life.

*****

Whenever I watched *To Kill a Mockingbird* with my high school students after reading the book, I'd get this strange, other-worldly feeling of being catapulted back in time. Like the film, it is a black-and-white world that I remember, documented in Polaroid snapshots and Super-8 films. Only certain colors from that time present themselves to me. The 1950-something Chevy that my sister nicknamed Poopsie, gray in photographs, revs up in my head in all of its pumpkiny-orange splendor. The swirly green leaves of the living room wallpaper seem to dance in the breeze of the window fan, though the pictures only preserve their black outlines. The three sets of shutters, photographed black against the stark white shingles of our little house on McKinley Drive, were really a sapphire blue, framing our windows with a splash of color uncharacteristic of both my parents and the neighborhood. But that's all. The rest, in my mind, is as gray as Maycomb.

Like Scout's, my memories of elementary school are vague. There are highlights that linger, of course, of those seven years, like singing in spring concerts, day-tripping to Sturbridge Village, wearing our Brownie uniforms on Tuesdays, tolerating trombone lessons, watching rockets being shot into space on the school's one TV, getting a coveted spot on the Safety Patrol and hearing from our principal (ironically named Miss Kennedy) that President Kennedy had been killed and that we should go directly home. We walked to and from school regardless of the weather (except on one particularly cold day when the neighborhood funeral director picked us all up in his hearse), and we wore little dresses with smocking all school-year round, accessorized with snow pants and cardigan sweaters in winter. Sometimes there was so much snow piled along the streets that our mothers could only pick us out by the colors of the pom-poms on the tops of our hats. No one came in cars to pick us up because most of our mothers didn't drive and even if they did, we were one-car families and our fathers took that one car to work. So we got ourselves to school and back, twice a day—home for lunch at noon and back to school by one—rain or shine, heat wave or blizzard, never thinking there might be any other way. Between all this coming and going were seven obligatory hours of instruction that are as nebulous in my memory as steam.

Summers were a different story. I have vivid memories of summer days. Like Scout and Dill and Jem, we were expected to be self-sufficient. Our daytime entertainment was our responsibility as long as it was outside and didn't involve anything that would interrupt our mothers' morning housework or afternoon soap operas. Houses belched out children after breakfast, expected them back for lunch, and booted them out again for the afternoon. The car in the driveway meant that it was time for supper and the streetlights were everyone's signal to hightail it home before dark. (Don't make me have to call you.) Bath, TV, snack, bed, start it all again. This was freedom.

In between meals our days were filled with running, hopscotch, bike-riding, make-believe, drawing, raiding gardens, waiting for the Good Humor man, playing with bugs and creating culinary concoctions from dirt and leaves and flower petals. The heat of the day was spent on a blanket under some tree or other drinking Kool-Aid, playing board games and reading Archie comics or books like *Cherry Ames, Student Nurse, Nancy Drew* and *Harriet the Spy.* We collected Japanese beetles in mayonnaise jars from the rose bushes and my grandmother would drown them in the watering can. The boys across the street had a picnic table at the edge of an enormous sandbox. We jumped from that table into that sandbox a million times—as paratroopers, astronauts, secret agents from U.N.C.L.E, deep-sea divers, ship-wreck survivors, Wile E. Coyote or Mary Poppins. Adults did not interfere in our play. I was always dirty.

We were unaware of the Cold War. We lined up on the curb in our jammies to watch Sputnik fly across the night sky with the same anticipation we felt when we waited for the ice cream truck. We giggled when someone said Bay of Pigs. We never watched the news. The Civil Defense signs on the school buildings and the Saturday morning Emergency Siren tests were just there, like air. We didn't question them. We also didn't question the fact that there were plenty of African-American kids in town, but none of them went to our elementary school.

There was stuff going on out there. Viet Nam was brewing, men were in space, global obliteration was possible, racism was as rampant as ever, and, by the time we got to high school in a few short years, the world as we knew it would blow wide open, politically, socially, ethically. Our innocence, like Scout's, was about to be challenged in ways that we were unprepared for, starting at home. My excitement at finding an African-American friend in our integrated junior high school turned to confusion when my mother, seeing us riding bikes together through our neighborhood, came out and told me to get my ass home. She said later that I had embarrassed her. I know now that my new friend was much more aware of what happened that day than I was. She was cordial to me after that, but nothing more. There was no Atticus Finch on McKinley Drive to teach us how to navigate these murky waters.

*****

In *To Kill a Mockingbird*, Harper Lee showed us how people lived in her world. She also gave me an insight into mine. Interestingly, though the book was published in 1960, I am not aware of its introduction into the curriculum of my school district while I was a student there. I could have used a dose of its wisdom. Despite the distance of space and time, Lee's story was apparently too close to home.

It was not until many years later, when I became a teacher myself, that I came to know and love the book and its message. Even now, after years of reading and rereading the book and viewing and reviewing the film, I can still look into the mirror that Lee waves in my face and think deeply about a lot of things. That's what good art does. My world is a better place because of it.

Saving *Your* Life

- Keep a log of the books that you read (or films that you watch) from now on. For each one, jot down a few reasons that it speaks to you. Does it remind you of yourself at a particular time in your life? Did it make you see something in an entirely new way? Did it teach you a lesson about life that you want to pass on? Who would you recommend this book (film) to?

- What might a reader learn about you from reading (viewing) the items on your list?

- Write "When I was a Kid…" across the top of a blank page in your journal. List all the things that come to mind. Don't be fussy. Leave extra pages blank for ideas that will come to you later. You'll be surprised by what you'll remember once you get going. Pick one or two vivid recollections and elaborate on them.

- Make a list of ways that your life has been enriched by literature and/or film.

- Imagine your life without your favorite book or film. What might change?

- What do we hope we are teaching our children? What are they actually learning from us?

- Which of life's biggest questions presented themselves to you as a child? How have you dealt with them over time?

- Did anything else about this essay remind you of your own experiences? In your notebook, jot down one memory, thought or opinion that popped into your head as you were reading.

What Teachers Do

I was being called back into action.

A friend in charge of a writing conference for high school kids wanted me to conduct a Creative Nonfiction workshop—if I was interested in getting back into the fray. No problem! Retirement has softened my edges a bit, but I still have what it takes to do the teacher thing. Besides, the task at hand was not at all daunting to an old pro like me. I would present two sessions of the workshop, attend a brief sharing session and be done. If this were a school day from my past life, it would be a mere two-fifths of one work day. In by nine—out by noon. What could be easier? Bring it on!

It had been two years since I prepared a lesson. I hadn't taken charge of a class since my retirement, but I wasn't concerned. Planning a class is (dare I say it?) like riding a bicycle. You just have to hop right on and get down to it. But, like anything else, when you haven't ridden in a while, the skill may still be there and the spirit may be more than willing, but the muscles, neglected and flabby, might have another idea. You may pedal enthusiastically down the driveway. You may even punctuate your ride with an exuberant fist pump or two, but it won't be long before your legs ache and your breathing becomes labored and you start to wonder whose body you're in.

As it turns out, lesson planning is a lot like that. While I knew what I had to do, doing it was another story. Creative Nonfiction is a giant genre with a zillion facets and I could have gone in as many directions. I had to find that one small thing out of so many possibilities that students could absorb, digest, practice and benefit from—all in one hour. I worked all day on crafting a lesson that suited me. I was amazed at how long it took to determine my focus, choose my materials and structure my presentation for a single one-hour session. In my prime, I could have planned a whole week's worth of classes in the time it took me to plan just that one, with time left over to grade some papers and call a few parents.

And, if my planning was this rusty, what could I expect of my actual presenting skills? Out of fear, I built a handout that would be self-guiding—to serve as my teleprompter in case my lesson flew out of my head when I stood up in front of the class. Everything that I wanted my students to leave with was there so that if I babbled or rambled or blathered or strayed or passed out cold on the floor, at least they would leave with a readable outline of what I *meant* to say and the morning would not be a total loss.

The sessions went just fine. As I had hoped, walking into a classroom full of kids was like going home and, once I was in the moment, I knew just what to do. I felt comfortable and prepared—or, most likely, comfortable *because* I was prepared. The kids were great—fresh-faced, attentive and excited to be meeting a real writer. Little did they know that I was just a teacher in writer's clothing. Just a teacher like the ones they see every day. Nothing special. Not really.

I taught English for thirty-six years before becoming a writer.

During that time I planned and taught five classes a day for a hundred and eighty days a year. That's approximately 32,400 classes, give or take a few for maternity leaves and graduate school and scheduling experiments and mental health days. And even if I wasn't there to teach my classes myself, I was still responsible for planning them and making sure that instruction went on with as little interruption as possible. All part of the job. Nothing special.

Imagine if all of those 32,400 classes took the same amount of effort that this one workshop took me. The mastery of the material. The determination of what was important. The alignment of the lessons to the standards of the day. The chewing it up in child-sized portions, like a mother bird, so that the kids could take it in and be nourished by it in the short period of time we had together. The nuts and bolts of organizing and structuring and typing and duplicating. The nerve-wracking self-doubt and the personal investment of time and energy. Good grief! Imagine if I went through all of *that* 32,400 times!

Oh. Wait.

I did.

Just like every other teacher who ever lived.

There's something about the teaching personality that makes people think that what teachers do is easy. A good teacher in his or her classroom looks comfortable, at ease, at home. But what students (and parents and politicians) don't see is the herculean behind-the-scenes effort—the preparation teachers put into every single working day to make sure that classes are relevant and interesting and interactive and meaningful.

It took this rusty old girl one whole day to plan one hour of good instruction. At that rate, every school day would have taken me a week to plan. But they didn't. Practicing teachers, out of necessity, will do it much quicker. But it doesn't mean that they do it with any less care. It is all that intellect and all that expertise and all that emotion and all that devotion compressed out of necessity, like a zip file, because teachers learn early that time is not their friend. But it's hard to understand the stamina this requires when even teachers sell themselves short. I didn't appreciate until I stepped away from the profession just how much is involved in what teachers do—in what I did 34,200 times. When you do it every day, you don't think of it as anything special.

Now I know better.

Saving *Your* Life

- Think of the best teacher you ever had. What was so special about him or her?

- Think of the worst teacher you ever had. What was he or she lacking? Would you change your assessment today?

- Would you make a good public school teacher? What important teaching skills do you have—or lack?

- Make a list of the things that you think all teachers should be able to do.

- Write about someone you know or appreciate who makes his or her work look easy. Is it easy work? What might it have taken this person to achieve this level of ease?

- What do you do so well that it looks easy? What did it take you to get to that point?

- Choose one activity, subject, job or skill that you would be qualified to teach to someone else. Now break it down into lessons and practice sessions that a beginner could digest.

- Think of an activity that you haven't done in a while. What would it take for you to regain your previous facility? Could you do it?

- Is there anything that you used to do that you just can't do anymore? What happened?

- Did anything else about this essay remind you of your own experiences? In your notebook, jot down one memory, thought or opinion that popped into your head as you were reading.

The Sycamore

My yard is full of trees. Oaks, maples, cedars, hemlocks, flowering varieties—some of the more decorative among them were planted by previous owners of the house, but most of them were just here and date back, I'm sure, to when my whole neighborhood was part of a deep, lush forest. I am happy to have them.

Big trees, though, create their share of yard maintenance issues and their wild, gyrating dances can be scary when storms hit. But what would this yard be without their cool shade and brilliant color? Their funky assortment of flowers, nuts, fruits, berries, seed pods and pine cones? Their coteries of birds and squirrels and chipmunks?

Well, it would be neater. And quieter.

And much less beautiful.

When we first moved into this house, I was unschooled in the ways of trees. The more I observed them, the more I was convinced that they were all dying. It was early November, so the annual autumnal shutdown was well underway. It was much more dramatic than I ever expected and sort of scary. I lived in New England all my life and I *knew* what trees did to prepare themselves for the winter. But I must admit that I never spent much time watching it happen. So, when, upon closer inspection, it looked like my new yard was imploding, I worried about what we were in for.

All summer, as we were negotiating and inspecting and planning our purchase of this property, the grove of fir trees in the side yard stood tall and strong and impervious to weather. Now, along with many wreaths' worth of pinecones—which I expected—the gigantic firs dropped a blanket of acidic yellow needles—which I did not. Wait. What? Was this normal? Were there enough needles left on the tree to keep it alive? Does the word ever*green* mean nothing here?

Walking further back, near the stream, I swished through acorns and hickory nut casings, certain that this was the feeding ground for every squirrel in town. Would this happen every year? Would the critters damage the trees? And what about all those knot holes? Were they signs of decay, despair and imminent demise?

But when I got to the big tree by the stream, the one that looked like two trunks growing from the same roots, the crunching beneath my feet sounded less swishy. Instead it crackled, like breaking plywood, as if I were doing damage with each step. I was startled to see that I was indeed walking on large sheets of fallen bark. I looked up and saw that the whole double trunk was mottled in several shades of gray and white. This was more than just interesting coloration. This was the bark peeling right off and falling where I stood. Clinging flaps of bark loosened in the slightest breeze. The spiraling race of a pair of squirrels could strip that trunk bare.

Great, I thought. Tree leprosy. We had this house inspected for a thousand things before we bought it. Never did it occur to us to bring in a tree expert. And now I had balding fir trees, a squirrel-besieged hickory, holey oaks and a gigantic, skinless whatever-it-is about to die at my feet.

I knew that this erstwhile beautiful yard was doomed.

Winter set in and the fir trees seemed to hold their own against the elements. The hickory dropped the rest of its nuts and the oaks threw down a mountain of acorns and then the squirrels left them alone. But the sycamore, as I learned it was called, just looked the same—grey and white and patchy. I started to look around town to see if other trees were experiencing similar distress. I discovered several motley-barked trees on my daily drive to work and I watched them all winter. They seemed to be doing exactly what my tree was doing. I reasoned that they couldn't all be dying and I relaxed some.

Spring is slow in coming to New England, so I had months to wait for the trees to resume living. Dormancy seems like such a waste of precious time, but winters can be hard here leaving much of nature little choice but to shut down. So you'd think that even trees would leap at the first chance to shake off the bleakness and start stepping out. Most of them did. But when it was nearly the end of June and the sycamore was still struggling to turn green (and still losing bark), I knew that death was looming. I peered through the blinds of the upstairs bathroom window first thing each day to see if it was still standing. I looked for tree-removal services in the Yellow Pages because I was certain that any day now it would fall like a giant beanstalk across the yard and I wanted to be prepared.

It never did. By mid-July, the sycamore had a full canopy— enormous leaves like King Kong hands. And it held onto them, just like all the others, well into the fall when they turned yellow and brown and drifted down to mix with maple reds and hickory oranges and the yellow acidic pine needles—and the grey bark. It took me a whole year to realize that I needn't have worried. But I'm glad I did. It made me watchful.

That sycamore held a few more surprises for me over the next twenty years—like the spring that it popped out pint-sized, premature leaves only to kill them and drop them and grow a new batch of beautiful big ones—all by the Fourth of July. It has withstood droughts and floods, squirrels and woodpeckers, blizzards and hurricanes. Right now, it hangs stubbornly on to a huge, wishbone-shaped branch that broke off from its top during Hurricane Irene. "The Widow Maker" has straddled and locked itself on to another branch some two stories up where it has been ever since. We thought one of the crazy, mutant super-storms that we've had over the last few years would have jarred it loose, but it hangs on like a prize-winning bronco buster. I watch it every day from the second-floor window next to my desk. It pivots and sways on its fulcrum showing no signs of releasing itself. It is a lesson in arboreal engineering. A natural wonder of my world.

This relationship that blossomed out of ignorance and worry has grown into one of patience and trust. It took me a whole year to learn what sycamores do. Over the years that followed, I have come to understand that sturdiness and strength underlie all of its idiosyncratic behavior. I no longer worry about its well-being.

I expect it.

Saving *Your* Life

- Watching anything over time will help you to become more aware of the world and your place in it. Tracing a tree through its seasonal cycles will not only make you more observant, but it will also help you to appreciate the part that the tree plays in your life. So, pick one tree. Make it your friend. Visit it regularly. Write about the relationship.

- If you live in the city, plant a seed in a pot that you can put on your windowsill and keep track of its progress. Making time to watch and understand the natural cycle of one thing can help to slow your busy life down a bit— enough to see how satisfying it is to pay attention to something outside of yourself, focus and record your observations.

- Pick one natural occurrence that you can trace over time. Keep a record of how it plays out in your world. Keep it to one thing, watch it closely and write down your observations. Rainfall or snowfall amounts, species of birds that come to your feeder and their pecking order, the feeding habits of a familiar critter, temperature, seasonal cycles of a plant or tree, weeds in your lawn, a daily cloud report, sun/cloud ratios—there are lots of possibilities!

- If you have a pet, watch and record its behavior over a week—maybe for a half an hour or so every day. You may think you know Fido or Boots or Polly or Nemo very well, but a close observation is sure to hold some surprises for you. You may also find that it's addictive!

- Do you have experience with the care and feeding of flora or fauna? Save your knowledge in an essay, journal or list that will simultaneously educate and impress your peeps.

- What natural wonders exist in your world? I'm not talking about geysers or waterfalls or volcanoes. I'm talking about birds and flowers and critters and trees. What backyard marvels have you observed? Write about the seven natural wonders of *your* world.

- Keep a seasonal photo log of one, small, specific nearby place. After a full cycle of seasons has gone by, compare the pictures and write about the physical changes that have happened. Describe them so that others can experience them, too.

- Did anything else about this essay remind you of your own experiences? In your notebook, jot down one memory, thought or opinion that popped into your head as you were reading.

Both Sides Now

I saw a film today.

The Teen-Aged Army declared war and deployed their troops.

The film, made by a college freshman as a class assignment, was sent to me by the filmmaker's proud dad. It is a deceptively simple scene—father and son in a tavern playing backgammon and discussing the events of the day. The conversation turns to Big Papi.

Sigh.

Baseball. Really? I don't care about baseball. I care even less about guys sitting around *talking* about baseball. I check the time bar at the bottom of the screen. The whole piece is only four minutes long. I continue watching out of courtesy.

Then I notice something. While the actors are talking, the camera is talking, too. A subtext begins to emerge and suddenly this little film has absolutely nothing to do with baseball.

Now I'm interested.

When it ends, I watch it again. I am simultaneously impressed by the quality of the filmmaking and troubled by the theme that emerges from it.

Should Papi stay or should Papi go? That is the question. But the more the beleaguered father in the film makes his case for "stay," the more the son, the man of the future, the naïve, arrogant, know-nothing, know-everything, blinded-by-his-own-inexperience son-of-a-bitch *kid* laughs it off with a shrug—as if to say, "What do *you* know, Daddy-O?"

While Dad uses words like "loyalty" and "leadership" and "look what he's done" and "a lot left in him," the boy speaks of "making room" for new players and being "past his prime" and old people being too greedy to know when to quit. His impertinence leaks out through his body language. He says things like, "He's got to realize, he's done," as if this mere boy has an inside track on the ways of the world and the nuances of the game that Papi does not. At one point, the boy actually uses the word "naïve" to describe a professional man twenty years his senior. How could he know?

And Dad, exasperated, runs out of arguments. His last, best retort is that Papi better watch his back around these younger players.

Boy wins. But only because his own disarming innocence makes him bold.

Serendipitously, I picked up the newspaper and glanced at a column written by a young mother-journalist who is young enough to be my daughter. The article describes the busy life of the modern working mother. So unique, she thinks. So utterly different from anything that came before, she explains. She is convinced that her experiences as a working mother bear no resemblance to the experiences of the working mothers of a generation ago. How does she know her life is different from what mine was twenty years ago? Was she there? Shouldn't *I* be the judge of how much things have changed? Or haven't? I, after all, am the only one of the two of us who has been in both places.

Bob Dylan wrote "The Times They are A-Changin'" when he was twenty-two. What did he know about adult life then? Really?

No more than the rest of us did at that age. But in our youth we all sang along with Dylan and his fellow troubadours and turned deaf ears to our parents—as all generations have with theirs before and since. I once sang Dylan's song like an anthem. It gave me a sort of pseudo-strength and a fabricated sense of power. It is the empowerment that comes with not knowing what you don't know. Ignorance *is* bliss. It's what makes people put themselves out there, take a risk, make it new. It's a developmental stage that we all go through.

Here on the other side, it's just so infuriating when we see our kids waving their ingenuousness in our faces like flags, when we know their experiences are not as different from our experiences as they think they are, when we can save them from themselves because we've *been there.*

And they don't listen.

We have all been *there*, too.

When I was in the eighth grade, the rock-opera *Hair* was all the rage. I bought the album and memorized all the songs, many about sex and drugs, the love anthems of the late 1960s. When my mother overheard the music, she was horrified. Among the lovely songs like "Good Morning, Starshine" and "Aquarius" and "What a Piece of Work is Man" were tucked songs with titles like "Hashish" and "Sodomy." I knew that "Sodomy" was a great song because of the way it made my mother's eyes go wide when she heard it.

I didn't know what any of it meant, but I was of the age when all I wanted to do was to declare myself separate and superior to my old-fashioned parents. This album, according to my inflated adolescent ego, put me in my own category. The subjects weren't anything new to any adult. They were just abrasive and hard to hear. These are words that people *still* don't use in polite conversation. But how would I know that? They were new to me. My innocent assumption was that they were new to everyone.

Keep up, Mom.

One day I had some friends over, so, of course, the first thing I did was to rev up my new album. My mother told me, in front of my friends, to turn it off. I gathered up my peeps, put the album in its sleeve and then under my arm and we stormed like a small platoon out the door.

When I was safely outside, I turned to my mother who was standing in the doorway, waved the album cover in the air and yelled, "Consider yourself educated!" My friends laughed and we ran down the street.

I was thirteen.

My mother didn't speak to me for days. Looking back, I don't know how she resisted breaking both of my legs.

Still, there was nothing, *nothing* she could have said that would have made me see her side because I hadn't been over there yet. It was my inadequacy, not hers.

It takes a long time to get over to that other side. Problem is, I didn't even know it was there. Nor did I for quite some time after the *Hair* debacle. At twenty-one, I loved being a student teacher armed with new methods that I thought were far superior to those used by my experienced mentors—until I got in the trenches myself and saw how flimsy they were. After graduation, I loved being chosen over older teachers for jobs—until it occurred to me many years later that young teachers are desirable not because they are more talented but because they are less expensive.

Now we see some young celebrities who believe that they are brave, cutting edge, so twenty-first century. In reality, they are commodities, money-makers. They are not the first young people to be manipulated and exploited by those older and smarter and they won't be the last. It will just take them a while to know that they were never really calling the shots. But don't try to tell them now. They can't hear you. We hope they see it before they've done too much damage to themselves.

I watch kids allow their lives to be swallowed in new technology and I lament what it takes from them. But I cannot tell them what they've lost by replacing books and personal observations with screens. They can't hear me. They truly believe that a life without a computer in your pocket is a life not worth living. They'll shoot knowing glances to one another to prove to themselves that they are the new insiders and that the world is their oyster and that I am obsolete.

But they'll know the feeling, someday, when they are fighting a losing battle against their own irrelevance, or when, as adults, they know that what their kids see as a gain is really, on some other level, a loss. Maybe a big one. And they will have no power to change it.

Should Papi stay? Maybe not. His experience is only useful for those who can hear him. When we've reached the age where our kids think they have more to teach us than we have to teach them, it's time to let them go off and make their own mistakes. We can only sit on the sidelines and nod perceptively.

We knew it would turn out like this. We have seen both sides. We told you so. We told you so.

But they will never listen. They can't. Just like we couldn't. It's not possible to know what you don't know until you know it. Until you've lived it. The ultimate frustration of parents is that they will always know more than their kids can understand. Always. And their kids aren't equipped to hear them any more than they can hear a dog whistle. It's not their fault. It's just the way it is.

I know this. I've been on both sides.

So, while old people know all about being young, young people will never, ever know anything about being old. They will never catch up. Until they are old themselves. And we are gone.

And all of this started because of a film I saw today—made by a very wise young man.

Oh boy.

Saving *Your* Life

- Good art makes us think. Write about the last thing you saw or read or viewed that made you think deeply about how life is.

- Write about an incident where it was obvious that you and your parents (or you and your children) were not on the same page.

- Write about a time when you looked at young people today and criticized their attitudes.

- Write about a time when you were young and older people criticized your attitude.

- In the 1960s the mantra was, "Never trust anyone over 30." What are your views on this today?

- It has been said that there are no young cynics or old idealists. Do you agree?

- Think of an example of technology that you can't live without that was not available to your parents. What have you gained? What would your parents say you lost? Does it matter to you?

- Think of an example of technology that kids today can't live without that was not available to you growing up. What have they gained? What do you think they've lost? Would they agree? Would they care?

- Think of someone who stayed at the party longer than they should have—a performer, a writer, a teacher. What were the results?

- Should Papi stay?

- Did anything else about this essay remind you of your own experiences? In your notebook, jot down one memory, thought or opinion that popped into your head as you were reading.

When a Writing Teacher Becomes a Teaching Writer

or

It's About Time I Learned My Lesson

I taught essay-writing to high school and college students for thirty-six years. I learned a lot about writing by teaching it. But that's nothing compared to what I learned about writing by doing it.

For most of my life, the writer in me earned her keep as the teacher's indentured servant. She practiced her craft by writing comments on student essays, emails home to parents, reaccreditation reports to the New England Association of Schools and Colleges, curriculum, curriculum, more curriculum, director's notes, play programs, guidance forms, disciplinary referrals, lesson plans and mind-numbing, underappreciated and dumpster-destined grunt work that all teachers abhor.

There were satisfying tasks as well. The "teacher me" used the "writer me" to produce some very fine supplemental materials and student handouts, if I do say so myself. But even the finest of handouts in the possession of fifteen-year-olds live short, tumultuous lives. Much of the writer's best work wound up in paper shredders, back-pack black holes and waste paper baskets.

Now that I have retired from teaching, I have finally given the writer the freedom to be. She has a room of her own and time to explore.

Some of what she produces is still dumpster-bound. But a lot of it is worth saving—and sharing. And, by *doing* all of this (instead of just thinking about it, talking about it or wishing it were so), I have discovered some things about the writing process—*my* writing process—that I didn't know, things that might be useful to others who are contemplating a similar path.

And, because old teachers never die, I am compelled to list my discoveries on a convenient, easy-to-read handout.

Here goes.

Twenty Lessons I Learned About Writing By Writing

1. Deadlines are everything.

It was a blog that gave me the incentive I needed to write regularly. Though I publish less often now, for a year I wrote and published a new essay every week. It primed the pump, kept me at it when it was hard and proved that I could do it. At the end of that year, I had fifty-two essays to my name.

Even without a blog, writing requires a calendar and a goal. Every writing project I undertake needs a time-line. Without a self-imposed deadline, I'd find a million other things to do.

2. Writing can be hard.

I used to think that good writers wrote effortlessly. Now I know that the opposite is true. Good writing takes work—and time. It can be a breeze one day and torture the next. Its fickleness is what makes it so compelling. For me, writing only happens if I buckle down and stick it out. It's like life—quitting is not an option.

3. I can write about anything if I sit there long enough.

If I pick a topic, focus on it and block out everything else, that topic will perform. This book is proof. If I commit and give a topic all the time it needs, an essay *will* emerge.

4. Staring out the window is part of the process.

But not too long. There's a fine line between contemplating and procrastinating.

5. Ideas are everywhere.

I've discovered that my real writing problem is that I have too many essay ideas to choose from and not too few. And this is not really a problem unless I use it as an excuse to procrastinate—which I do. This is when I flip a coin, commit to ONE idea, focus and trust Lesson #3.

6. Every idea is a topic worth trying out.

No idea is too lame if it means something to you and if it's honest. Once again, see #3. It hasn't failed me yet.

7. It helps to be a good technician, but it's only part of the game.

There are two concerns here—what you say and how you say it. I have always been a good technician. That's why I became an English teacher. I have only recently discovered that I might actually have something to say. That's why I became a writer.

8. *I have more stories than I thought.*

So do you. You're alive. You have stories to tell. Lots of them. You'd better get started. You'll be amazed at how quickly the list will grow. Focus. Set a deadline. Go.

9. *If my stories are well-told, other people will relate to them— even the ones that I think are ordinary.*

We like to know that we share experiences with others. It has surprised me to find how readers react to my work. While we love reading about people whose experiences are unique or bizarre, we mostly like reading about people with whom we can relate. It makes us feel like we belong somewhere. My favorite moments are when readers tell me that something I wrote reminds them of their own stories.

10. *Memories are there. When I started looking for them, I started finding them.*

It's funny how memories hide from you—until you start looking for them. It's like walking into a room and having everyone you've ever known jump out and yell, "Surprise!" But, the party can't start until you open the door. That's the signal. Until then, all those memories will just have to sit quietly in the dark.

11. *It's all about the revision—up to a point.*

Here's where the technician comes in. Once an English teacher, always an English teacher. I read and reread, edit and re-edit. Still, I find mistakes and weak spots. And, what's worse, sometimes I don't find them at all. But I am learning that sometimes excessive revision is just another excuse to not start that new piece because polishing an old piece to death is much easier than starting something new.

12. *Writing happens as you are writing.*

I can "think it through" until my head explodes, but until I start writing, I have no idea how (or if) it will turn out. It is the act of writing itself that drives the direction of a piece. Unless you are clairvoyant, you have no idea how a piece will turn out if all you do is think about it. You have no choice but to jump in, *get started* and hope for the best. Writers write. Period.

13. *Trust the process.*

I had to learn this as a teacher, too. My teen-aged "audience" would bring brilliance out of me that I didn't know was there and that I couldn't have planned and that wouldn't have happened without them in the room. I learned to expect the unexpected every day, to trust that the planets would align and good things would emerge when all the parts were in place.

Writing is the same. Get all the parts together, set them in motion and let them work. Have faith in your story and take the leap. It's sort of like walking a tightrope without a net. You either commit all the way or you don't. It's so much better when you do. In other words, do it. Write. See what happens. It's the only way.

14. *Blogs and books have readers. You never know who or where or when. Be there for them.*

My regular blog readership is small but loyal. Many of them

are family and friends. But I also have had visitors from all over the world. I don't know who they are, how they found me, why they have come or if they will ever visit again. So, while I have them, I am responsible for giving all of them the best read I can. Even if they just visit once. Even if it was by mistake.

15. Writers must create time and space in which to work.

This is harder than it sounds. But time and space are as important to the creative process as ideas and words. Finding time is up to you. Without it, you cannot create. Space doesn't have to be fancy. It just has to be yours. Think Virginia Woolf. My favorite spot is where I began writing my first blog—on my back porch. This is not a particularly welcoming place during a New England winter, so when it's cold I work inside—in a small, unadorned room, with a door.

16. Families must respect that time and place.

This is also much harder than it sounds, especially if there are kids involved. But if you want to be a writer, you must work it out. Start with a desk and a door. Learn to close it. I'm working on this.

17. The writing life can be isolating. Find some friends.

A writing class or conference can help. Especially after a long winter. Get out. Breathe the air. See what other people are doing. Get some advice. But not too much. Rejuvenation can morph to procrastination in a heartbeat if you let it. I am an expert on this.

18. A piece of writing tends to improve all by itself if you let it sit for a few days.

Sometimes I cry because what I am writing is so awful. But I've learned not to throw it away, at least not while I am in the throes of despair. There is something about a dark desk drawer and a few days' time that can work magic on what once was the worst thing I'd ever written. Maybe there are elves in there.

19. Most of the time, all you have to do is start.

I spent a lot of time reading books about writing. This was what I did instead of writing. I told myself that I was preparing to write and learning the ropes, but really I was afraid to start. It was easier to put off starting than it would be to start and fail. But then it occurred to me that, if I wanted to be a writer, I was a failure every day that I didn't write. Even writing badly is a measure of success, albeit small.

20. Sometimes the best writing happens when you start out to write about something else.

Time and again my writing goes in unexpected directions once I get started. Sometimes this is frustrating, but most of the time it is a gift. And it only happens *when I am writing*—not when I'm thinking about writing or wishing I were writing or planning to think about wishing I were writing. It is a gift that I get for actually starting—a bonus, a gold star, a pat on the back for a job well-done. It's another incentive to get past the hardest part—starting.

There you have it. Every writer learns about writing from

writing, so find a place, find the time, focus on a topic, tune out the world and DO IT.

Because you can.

And you should.

Saving *Your* Life

- My lessons appear here in random order. Pick your top five and write about how you relate to them.

- Pick five stories of your life that you would like to save forever. Put them in a list numbered 1-5.

- Sit down in a quiet place with whatever writing utensils you like and write Life Story Number One. Start at the beginning and don't stop until you have told the whole story. Don't worry about anything besides getting the details down in words.

- Work your way through your list. This could take a while. Carve out the time you need, focus on one story and write it until it is done. Save the next one for another day.

- Once you have written five stories of your life, make a list of all of the things you have learned about writing.

- Are you a procrastinator? Write about one thing that you have a tendency to put off. Why do you think you do this?

- I often wonder how kids today focus on anything. They have so many things vying for their attention every minute of the day. How do you tune out the world so that you can focus on the task at hand?

- What kinds of things are easy for you to concentrate on?

- What kinds of things are impossible for you to concentrate on?

- Write about a time when you just couldn't get a project off the ground. What became of it?

- Write about someone you've known who could get totally involved in a project. What kinds of behaviors did you observe in that person that the rest of us could use for getting things done?

- Did anything else about this essay remind you of your own experiences? In your notebook, jot down one memory, thought or opinion that popped into your head as you were reading.

Thanks, Shirley!

It had been an evening of drinking and loud reminiscing. Food was plentiful and people waved away seconds with one hand while they grabbed "just one more" with the other. I put a box of Zip-Loc bags on the counter and made it very clear that no one was allowed to leave without filling one with leftovers for tomorrow's lunch.

As we said goodbye to the last of the guests, I glanced out into my backyard. Judging by the number of empty beer bottles strewn about, the wine bottles in the recycle bin and the chairs askew in every possible way, it seemed that everyone had a really good time. It was a group of people that, for an assortment of reasons—age, distance, health—doesn't gather very much anymore. But it was good to know that when we do, the old sparks can still fly.

When everyone was gone, I went out back to start cleaning up. There were soda cans rolling around on the patio and assorted party debris littering the lawn. As I made my way across the grass, my flip-flops squished in I-really-don't-want-to-know-what. I'm hoping it was a sandwich.

It looked like we just threw a frat party.

But we didn't.

We threw a funeral.

*****

My mother-in-law was ninety. She had a wonderful life and even in her last few months of worsening dementia and cancer, she was surrounded by competent caregivers and loving family. And she deserved every one of them. She was a caregiver herself who had cultivated friendships, nurtured family and generated so much love and goodwill in her lifetime that everyone who knew her thought of her as a positive life force, proof that there was good left in the world. I never heard a critical word spoken about her and very few by her. If she criticized you, then you must have needed it.

Most of the friends and family from her generation were either already gone or too frail to travel. Even her younger brother was too ill to come. This is why funerals for the very elderly tend to be small affairs—immediate family and perhaps a few close friends of the children. But this was a life that had long arms—and everyone in my back yard that night had been hugged by them at one time or another.

And so they came—to mourn the death and to celebrate the life. Nieces, nephews, cousins, friends of her children and children of her friends came from New Hampshire, Connecticut, Massachusetts and Rhode Island. Grandchildren and great-grandchildren traveled from South Carolina, Virginia and Tennessee and skyped in from Wisconsin. The day that began with solemnity at the funeral home, that turned to grief at the memorial service and then to relief at the luncheon, ended in a party in my backyard—a group expression of the sheer joy that comes from being all together again.

We will miss Shirley very much. She was the sun at the center of our orbit. It is because of her that this circle of family and friends exists. It is because of her lifetime efforts to bring people together that lots of good parties happened—that *this* party happened. And it was fun. It would have been disrespectful to her if we had not enjoyed our time together. We sent her off that day with love and gratitude for all she did to make our lives better. I can't imagine that she would have wanted it any other way.

We can't change the fact that people we love die. We will die, too, and it did not escape many of us in the oldest of the three generations present that day that the death of our parents means that we are now next in line.

So let the party continue. We need it, all we can get of it, now more than ever. Those who passed ahead of us understood this, Shirley more than most. Her lesson to us is a simple one, and, as such, it is easy to forget. There is no better way to honor her memory than to be together. As often as we can. Preferably in the back yard with chocolate chip cake and beer.

Thank you, Shirley. You taught us what it means to love each other. We'll never forget you.

Life goes on even as lives come and go.
We save what we can and move on.

Saving *Your* Life

- Write about the last funeral you attended. What rituals were observed? Were you comforted by them? Would you have changed anything?

- How would you like your life to be celebrated after you're gone? Should it be a solemn affair? A wild party? Something in between? In an essay, a journal entry or a list, leave instructions.

- Write about the most fun you ever had at a funeral.

- Write about the most difficult funeral you ever attended.

- We grieve and remember in personal ways. Write about a loved one whom you have lost and how you dealt with it both at the time and since.

- Funerals are for the living. They give us an opportunity to gather, to grieve together, to say goodbye. They mark a moment from which we will then go forward. Write about different funeral rituals that you have experienced. Which ones were the most comforting and useful for *you*?

- Funerals also remind us of our own mortality. We humans all live with the knowledge that time is *not* on our side. How do you cope with this?

- Did anything else about this essay remind you of your own experiences? In your notebook, jot down one memory, thought or opinion that popped into your head as you were reading.

Part Seven
Musings

Ideas. We all have them. Most of the time. More than we can count.

But having them is easy. Catching them and using them is harder. It takes motivation, some effort and a plan. Mine starts with a little black Moleskine notebook. This notebook works like a fishing seine or a lobster pot or one of those backyard bird traps that kids build with a cardboard box, a stick and a string. It catches and stores ideas that flow from my head, to my hand, through a blue Pilot G2 fine-point gel pen and onto the page. But this can only happen if I make the effort to set the trap, check it periodically and collect up the contents. Once my ideas are gathered up and safely tucked away on the page, then it's up to me to ferret out the keepers and decide not only what to use, but also when and how. This is where the work of the writer begins—with a little black notebook full of ideas.

Musings are especially nebulous. To give them life, we have to snatch them out of our mental miasma and give them a body. For this we need words, written words, to provide substance and shape, like clay.

Catch your ideas in a little notebook. Choose those that move you. Give them life with words. Then mold and shape those words like sculpture to turn your musings into works that will live forever.

Each of the essays in this section was born from an idea that begged me for a body. I was only too happy to oblige.

Educide

There once was a principal whose motto was, "Hire the best people you can. Then, stand back and let them do their jobs." He stood by that philosophy for a long time, observing often, intervening when necessary, listening always. He was practical, approachable, visible and open to new ideas. He trusted his teachers and they respected him. The school hummed.

No one knew it at the time, but he turned out to be one of the last of the old-fashioned, hands-on, roll-up-your-sleeves, we're-all-in-this-together, practitioner principals. Sadly, there were changes in the wind that would render his style obsolete and usher in, well, a divorce.

And when teachers and administrators parted ways, it seems that they parted for good.

It started when school administrators disconnected themselves from their teaching roots. They were encouraged by theorists (and, it would seem, school boards) to abandon their roles as teachers and champions of teachers and become, instead, Educational Leaders. They went to the mountaintop and returned with ideas the likes of which, they assumed, mere classroom teacher-mortals had never entertained. They became distant, aloof and arrogant. Instead of climbing down into the trenches and making themselves part of a team, they preferred to set their sights higher—to commune not with practitioners, but with *experts*. Soon they believed themselves to be among them.

We classroom teachers, on the other hand, armed with our own advanced degrees and years of experience, were loath to give up our practical, *successful* methods for those of the publish-or-perish (aka flash-in-the-pan) theorists. We were told, then, that we needed to experience a paradigm shift in order to embrace an assortment of educational panaceas that would magically transform our profession. We needed to continue doing what we were doing, but we just needed to do it, well, differently, incorporating the theories of every doctoral dissertation that came down the pike. Not that what we were doing was bad or wrong. It just wasn't trendy. It needed to be *aligned*, you see, with a certain pyramid of *standards*, you see, so that our students will make *progress* according to certain measurable *criteria*, don't you know, determined by, as far as we were concerned, aliens from the Zone of Proximal Development. Maybe what we did already worked, but it wasn't *fashionable*. It didn't have a *name*. Most of us incorporated a lot of new ideas into our daily practice regularly—the parts that made sense and helped our kids. We just didn't know what to call it besides good teaching. We felt that we were being sold a bill of goods—a cure-all for an illness we didn't have, the kind that would rot the enamel off of our teeth if we weren't careful.

But, when theories became mandates and got dropped in our laps in the forms of controlled lesson planning and "creative" grouping and experimental schedules, we had no choice but to muddle through on our own. And so we did. We had to. No amount of promised "support" can follow you into your classroom. You are the whole show. When you walk into a classroom every day and face your students, *you* are the expert and must live up to that. A teacher standing in front of a class lives or dies by the sharpness and quality of her wits, intelligence, skill and practical experience. Despite the upheaval, we faced our classes every day armed with a command of our subjects, a commitment to our purpose and a compassion for our kids. The rest of it happened or didn't depending on its usefulness. Theories be damned.

It boiled down to this. We loved our work. Our kids were successful. We worked hard, we were good at what we did and we would keep at it despite the annoying interference of the theorists.

And we were able to do that for quite some time, for the most part. Nod and smile in meetings and then go back to our classrooms, close our doors and do what we knew to be right. The stylings of theorists and the blind acceptance of administrators shook things up a bit, but we were able to adjust, play the game and still do our jobs. It wasn't the first time this sort of thing happened and we knew it wouldn't be the last. We would weather whatever storm of expert-theorist-administrator came our way. The winds always died down eventually.

They did this time, too—for a while. But as I look back I see that this was the beginning of the end of teaching as I knew and loved it. The storm that followed, supported by an air mass of self-serving Ed.Ds fulfilling their publication requirements, was about to become a tornado. And monitoring the front were the most dangerous storm-chasers of them all.

Politicians.

Like many school administrators and the "experts" who hoodwinked them, politicians with a stake in education served themselves by claiming to be able to fix things that weren't broken. Politicians never needed to set foot in a school building to know what they wanted. They are businesspeople. They court businesspeople. They work for and with businesspeople. The business of business is profit. And that's fine. We need that. But schools don't fit into a business model. Schools are nonprofit entities; we can't judge their worth in terms of numbers, though that is often where the discussion ends.

So what, then, is the business, the profit, the payoff of schools?

Teachers will say, among other things, "The nurturing of personal growth and self-worth, the development of life skills, the shaping of individuals into the best that they can be, the formation of relationships, memories and shared experiences, the creation of community, the fostering of an appreciation for art and literature and science and math, instilling curiosity and love of learning, cultivating an appreciation for the beautiful and an intolerance for the hateful, providing opportunities for kids to discover who they are and what they're good at, and helping them to step into their future with a plan that will ultimately build and insure the strength and well-being of America."

Politicians will say, "Test scores."

Passion, compassion and commitment? Sorry. No room for them on the spread sheet.

To that end we have No Child Left Behind, Race to the Top, Common Core, countless state, town and district plans with annoying acronyms, time-consuming evaluation plans, standardized (i.e. one size fits all) curriculum, administrative micromanagement, invasive oversight and enough standardized test preparation to fill a school year without ever getting to the actual curriculum. We have spread sheets and focus groups and percentiles and power point presentations and arrogant child-bosses and giant binders full of data.

Ah. Data. There it is. I've said it. The profession, it seems, was wallowing in failure for the last two hundred years while we waited for technology to catch up and give us what we in American education really, really needed—a way to gather and analyze massive quantities of data.

Sigh.

Now we can keep track of every possible activity that could ever be of interest (or not) to any party ever in the history of education. Since teachers are not statisticians (yet), most of our work in this regard is experimental and dangerously time-consuming. It robs time and energy from the real work. The things we are really good at, working *with kids* (Yeah, yeah. We know. Stop whining.), teaching our *subjects* (Really? That again?) are much more important, but, since there's no accurate way to measure how a good class discussion affected the lives of the kids in Period C, let's just keep our attention on the stats, OK?

So as we struggle with spreadsheets that might as well be written in ancient hieroglyphics, precious hours are squandered trying to quantify the unquantifiable. We spend planning and professional development time filling out forms, learning new programs to report out data, watching podcasts of "experts" who haven't seen the inside of a public school classroom in years (if ever), getting the IT guys down to fix equipment that even when brand new wasn't up to the job and taking our real work home to be done at the kitchen table while our spouses clean up from dinner and keep the kids quiet—again.

Well, after years of observation in the field, I, too, have a theory. All of this boils down to one thing.

No one in charge of teachers really knows how to evaluate them.

Teacher evaluation is a big part of an administrator's job and a politician's platform. That makes it a big, hairy, threatening monster under the bed. What do we do to big, hairy, threatening monsters under our beds?

We kill them.

The mountains of data being produced in our schools have less to do with student achievement than with teacher achievement—designed to strip it of the subjective, to purge it of the creative and to reduce it to a system that can be analyzed by machines.

This, too, has a history. In the 80s we began to hear rumblings of the importance of "teacher accountability." Interestingly, this coincided in some states with the passing of legislation that finally raised teachers' salaries to a living wage. People didn't like the idea that teachers could earn enough money to actually live on when they didn't even work in July. (No one paid attention to the fact that teachers work more hours from August to June than most other jobs do in a calendar year— without compensation.) So they started to question teachers' value—both in productiveness and in dollars and cents. Were teachers worth the extra money? (Funny, our work was more than satisfactory to the public when we were cheap.) Hmm.

Sounds like a platform brewing to support a new bandwagon. Elect me and I will make sure that those greedy teachers are earning your hard-earned tax dollars.

Teachers became the target, the latest in a long line of economic scapegoats, and it was amazing how many "tax-conscious" citizens picked up a slingshot. Encouraged, politicians and theorists and Ed.Ds and experts joined forces and had a field day.

And here we are. 2016. A classic case of "be careful what you wish for."

The avalanche of directives and mandates and testing requirements crushing us is a way to make it look like good teaching is an easily measurable thing. It's not. And, the new mandates have nothing to do with kids. They're a way to make people outside of the profession think that they can tell the good teachers from the bad by looking at their—data. Kind of like the way you'd buy a car. (Should that teacher's contract be renewed? Well, give her tires a kick, measure her wheelbase and check out her MPG. Then we'll talk.)

We are squeezing the life out of a career that is supposed to be all about making life better. Sit in any meeting that peddles data collection and focus groups and spread sheets. Watch the shoulders of the good teachers droop, their faces pale and their eyes glaze over with despair. Living, breathing, vibrant educators turn to stone the same as if they looked Medusa in the eye. It is best for them to shut up, tune out and get it over with—like naughty children being spanked.

But turn the topic over to *teaching kids*, and you can practically see their cheeks flush and their eyes dance and their faces come alive again.

Better yet, skip the meeting, stand back and let these people do their jobs and you just might witness brilliance.

But the meetings go on and the message to teachers is clear.

Test scores do not evaluate students. They evaluate schools and teachers. Badly.

We knew it all along.

By today's standards, a good teacher is someone who can insure that Johnny will reach an arbitrary, determined-by-who-knows-who level on the standardized test-du-jour. A good teacher is someone who dutifully fills out forms and collects evidence to prove that the job is getting done when that time would be better spent just doing the job. A good teacher nods resignedly when the "experts" arrive to turn his world upside down yet again.

If that's what they really want, teachers should give it to them. And nothing more. Reduce the teaching of their beloved subjects to ten-question, multiple choice quizzes. Grade them by machine. Get meaningless new grades online a minimum of three times a week to pacify parents. Suck the substance, the value and the joy right out of it. Go home at 2:30 with an empty bag. Have a life.

But they can't. Not the good ones. Because good teachers are artists. Artists do what they do because they are born to do it, not because there's notoriety or money or even appreciation involved. They do it because they love it and they see its inherent value. They're driven. It's who they are. They see their work as their small contribution to the continuation of the cosmos, their part in making sure humanity lives to see the sun rise another day. That is very difficult for a statistician to measure. It will never fit on those spreadsheets.

Many of the best teachers will crumble under the arbitrary demands of current programs. They are suffocating under the sheer mass of new mandates. Too much superfluous paperwork. Too much time diverted from the real work. Too many late nights. Too much debilitating oversight. Too much unmanageable, unyielding stress. They will quit or retire before their time so that they can maintain their health and their families and they will see it at as a personal failure.

I know. I am one of them.

Left in charge of our classrooms will be the literal, the unimaginative, the easily satisfied and those who will eagerly reduce the futures of our children and the careers of their teachers to numbers on a graph. They will get high scores. Our kids will wither in their care.

The solution? It's easy. Remember that principal from the beginning of this essay? He knew the answer all along—before the "experts" got their hands on him.

Hire good people. Then get the hell out of their way and let them do their jobs.

Saving *Your* Life

- You have been to school. What makes a good teacher?

- Think of times when you knew people were approaching a problem the wrong way. How did you react?

- Note other examples in your life of the battle between making money and making sense.

- Does your boss actually perform the same that job you do? Did he/she ever? How does that affect conversations you have with him/her about your work?

- Does your job satisfy you? Really? Is it what you were born to do?

- If not, what would you rather be doing? What keeps you from doing it?

- If you are not a teacher, imagine yourself in front of a classroom full of kids. You pick the age and grade and subject. Then write about your day.

- Sometimes we just need to blow off steam. Is there an issue that really bothers you? Write about the problem. Why does it exist? Who is perpetuating it? How would you change things if you could?

- Write about your favorite teacher. What were his or her strengths? How would you measure them? Are there some things about teacher performance that aren't measurable?

- Did anything else about this essay remind you of your own experiences? In your notebook, jot down one memory, thought or opinion that popped into your head as you were reading.

Untitled

An afternoon at the Guggenheim Museum in uptown Manhattan made me think about the nature of art.

On our many trips to New York City, the Guggenheim is a museum that we have neglected, rarely venturing further uptown than the Met. We always meant to give Frank Lloyd Wright's creation its own day, if only to enjoy the architecture and to experience working our way up the spiral like hermit crabs in a conch. So, on this day, as we had tickets for an 8 p.m. curtain and all afternoon to explore someplace new, we made our way to the Upper East Side.

The building itself is a piece of modern art. It is round and layered, like a cake. But each level increases slightly in circumference as it rises, like one of those collapsible cups you might take camping. It is white and plain and ironically interesting to look at in spite of its lack of embellishment. Its shape sets it apart so completely from the traditional high rises in the neighborhood that it could have been set down on the spot by aliens, not built from the ground up, but beamed down in its entirety in a moment, intentional and fully formed—a giant, intergalactic blender, perhaps, providing sustenance to space travelers after their long trip. It is as distinctive in its own way and as much fun to turn a corner and stumble upon as the Trevi Fountain or the Pantheon.

On the day we were there, the main exhibit was a collection by a group of modern young artists working in the 1950s and 1960s. We had no idea what this would include, being unfamiliar with this group of artists and their works. We had come here to experience the museum itself and its permanent collection of Impressionists. My tastes in art are rather eclectic and I do find them changing over time, but I have learned to appreciate skill and vision even if the actual work of art doesn't move me. I knew, then, that I would find something to like in any exhibit mounted by a museum with the Guggenheim's reputation.

Or so I thought.

Once we made our way through the crowded lobby and started up the spiral, we were diverted into an alcove dotted with a handful of pieces meant to serve as our introduction to the works that would challenge our senses for the rest of our stay.

I hated them.

They were, to me, pretentious, shallow and phony. They were self-righteous, arrogant and pompous. They were juvenile, silly and pointless. Their artists were trying so hard to be different, to be cutting edge, to cast off the old and to embrace the new, that they forgot that being new is not an artistic end in itself. They forgot that there is nothing new to be said. There are only new ways to say old things. Human things. Things that have existed for as long as humanity has. They forgot that artists don't create truth—they discover it.

I stepped out of that little room. I had just watched myself in a mirror, watching words being reflected across my face. I wondered how that giant dream catcher hanging from the ceiling was an improvement over anything that ten year olds make in summer camp. I watched a film of geometric shapes blur by too quickly for me to make meaning out of them. I jumped when a small, black box of disparate mechanical parts began to move. I saw a square canvas of yellow suspended from the ceiling next to a rectangle of white, disturbed only by a slightly diagonal black line. I saw other suspended canvases of neutral color that used wire and other material to create texture, making them only slightly more interesting. The artists' names were stenciled on the floor so as not to break vision, but it seemed more to me that they were there to make sure that you saw them.

"I hate this," I said to my husband, shocked first that I felt that way and second that I said it out loud. Then it felt pretty good. Once I allowed myself to own the feeling, I could view the rest of the exhibit with focus and confidence. I wasn't afraid to say that I didn't know what this or that piece meant. I was sure that, to me, it meant nothing.

The art world can be an intimidating place. If something is displayed in a museum, it has merit to someone, but that doesn't mean that it speaks to you. It also doesn't mean that you are a Yahoo if you are critical of it, as long as you are flexible and thoughtful and open in your approach. In other words, if you give it a chance, if you apply reasonable criteria to determine its value and you look for what the piece means to communicate, you're allowed not to like it.

Real art is a way of reaching out to, of making sense from or of finding a way in the world. It reveals and teaches and communicates. It requires skill and experience to do well. If notoriety follows, so be it. But if notoriety is the reason for it, then the work rings hollow.

In order for a work of art to speak to me, I have discovered over time, certain things must occur. First, I look for skill. Does this artist understand the medium in which he or she works? Film, writing, graphic arts, performance arts—all require an understanding of the elements of the medium. For most, that takes time and dedication. I want my artists to be good at handling their tools. I don't want to pay to see or hear things that I could do myself. Although it's not enough, proficiency is difficult and important and worthy of recognition.

Second, I look for vision. Does the artist have something that he or she is trying to say? Is there a search for truth? Have the elements of the medium been used to show depth of thought, to reveal something about who we are and how we live? I will happily acknowledge the value in that, even if I don't get it.

And finally, I look for artists who attempt to communicate with me. If a sculptor or painter or writer or filmmaker or musician is so esoteric that, despite my honest attempts, the truths that he or she has discovered (if any) are purposely obscure and undecipherable, I will look elsewhere. There's no reason to keep knocking on a door that's never going to open. If an artist doesn't enlighten me or please me or reach out to me, what's the point? Life is short.

So, my criteria by my side, I trudged upward through the spiral, past piece after piece of the collection. These artists, working during the 1950s and 1960s, saw the post-WWII era as an ending. They saw themselves and their work as a brand new beginning—typical of the youthful arrogance of the 1960s that I remember so well. Too young to know what I didn't know, I felt like we were making it new in the 60s, too, even though I had no idea what the old even was. What were we rebelling against? I didn't know. I only knew that rebelling was fun and, for me, fit right into the hormone-induced delirium that was junior high. As I look back I can see the explosion of the time—rock and roll music, Cold War hysteria, Viet Nam protests, political upheaval, loss of trust, drug use, campus unrest, parental distress, bizarre fashion statements—and how we could have mistaken it all as something unique. Fifty years later it is clearer to me that every generation, every movement, every era exists in its current form because it wants to distinguish itself from the generation, movement or era that preceded it. All behavior is reaction. It's not new. Nothing is new. Dressed differently, perhaps, but not new.

So, these young artists believed that they were ushering us into some nebulous tomorrow. And they were going to do it with abstraction and arrogance. With canvasses shot randomly with arrows and monochromes edged with nails. With bread glued to a board and painted white. With surfaces charred by flamethrowers and slashed by knives. With light on the walls and sand on the floor. With huge plastic disks, corrugated and mounted and set to go into motion on the hour. With giant black circles and bold arbitrary lines. With black and white and silver and reflection and darkness and movement. With shiny streamers suspended from the ceiling and surrounded by museum guards who won't let you get close enough to blow on them to see how their movement will reflect you.

And to make matters worse, many of the pieces in this collection are conspicuously titled "Untitled." This makes me angry. A title is a lifeline that an artist throws to a viewer or reader. It's a clue to the essence of a piece. It's a good-faith gesture. The lack of them in this exhibit made me feel that the artists don't understand any more about their work than I do. Or if they do, they feel no need to share it. Either way, it was insulting to me, especially coming from someone who wanted to catapult me into tomorrow.

There was a time when I would have nodded and approved and kept my disdain to myself. I would have believed that the fault was my own, that there was something lacking in me and that's why I didn't get it—like the grown-ups in "The Emperor's New Clothes" who won't admit that the Emperor is naked because they've been told that only special people can see the fine new robes and they don't want to publicize the fact that they are not among the chosen. Now, while I believe that I must make an effort and not just discount things that are new and unfamiliar, I also believe that it is the artist's obligation to meet me at the door.

I was relieved to step out of the spiral into an annex that housed the museum's Thannhauser Collection. Seeing the familiar brushstrokes of the Van Gogh was like slipping into a comfortable pair of jeans. The room was full of old friends—Monet, Pissarro, Rousseau, Toulouse-Lautrec, Picasso, Manet, Cezanne, Gauguin—all revered and reviled at one time for their newness. But unlike the bread or the plexiglass or the firestorms, these paintings still speak to me long after their newness has faded. While the more modern artists in the house thought that they could wipe the slate clean and start fresh, these artists, and others whose works live on, understand that we can't erase the past. We can only learn from it, understand how it works in us, and move on from there.

To shake off the past, we must first know it. Once we know it, we will see that it permeates who we are. We are the sum total of all who have come before. We can, perhaps, shape or overcome the past's influence, but only if we know it's there. We can react to it, but we can never escape it. It is what makes us human. This is the same for us as it was for the Elizabethans and the ancient Greeks and the indigenous peoples about whom we have no records.

This understanding is what makes Shakespeare and Twain and Picasso and Mozart so rich and enduring. Expressing old truths in new ways is what makes for art that lasts. The truth's the thing.

Was my day at the Guggenheim a bust? Not at all. I enjoyed the day very much. It made me think about things that matter to me—like the craziness that was the 1960s, the relationship between youth and age both among us and within us, the importance of art in our lives, the endurance of the past no matter how hard we may try to erase it, the necessity of understanding our place in the continuum and the dangers of taking ourselves too seriously or thinking that we have got it all over our predecessors.

And I am proud that I was bold enough not only to form and articulate an opinion that ran counter to the experts at The Guggenheim but also to believe that I am entitled to it. The art on display that day was there because museum professionals with much more artistic experience and knowledge than I saw its worth. I respect that. But there was a time when that fact would have intimidated any judgment right out of me. Now, we can both stand solidly behind our views and the artists can be proud of the thought and discussion that their work evoked.

I'd say an essay about a day like that deserves a title.

Saving *Your* Life

- There is a chance that I am completely off the mark here. After all, the venerable Guggenheim found this collection to be worthy of its attention. There may be something I missed or something that I don't know about the artists, their times and their lives that informs their art and their outlook. Maybe my opinion says more about my shortcomings than theirs. Write about something you dislike and decide what this reveals about you.

- Pick a painting by a famous artist that you especially like. Describe it and explain why it is meaningful to you.

- Set up a gallery of favorite paintings at the website of the Metropolitan Museum of Art. Whenever you need a writing idea, pick a painting and interact somehow with it. Enter it, chat with the subjects, bale hay with the farmers, weep at the graveside, dance with the party and write about your experiences. Or just describe it for someone who hasn't seen it and tell why it is meaningful for you.

- When your kids think they are the only ones in the world to feel a certain way, how do you assure them that they are not?

- Do you feel intimidated when you look at art in a museum? What do you look for when you look at a painting? Develop your own list of the things that a piece of art should have if it is to speak to you. Then, go to a museum and apply your criteria as you look at the artwork. Does your list hold up? Revise it until it does and then write an essay about how it works for you.

- Write about a time when you were offended by something but didn't say so for fear of looking stupid.

- Think back to the time in your life when you still knew everything. How was life for you in the days when you were certain that your parents were idiots?

- The teaching of history is taking a hit these days. How is your general knowledge of history? How has it helped/hurt you in your navigation of life today? Does it matter?

- How about your family history? What do you know about your ancestors? How does this affect your current life choices?

- If art was being cut from your town's public school curriculum, would you fight to save it? Why or why not? If there was a choice to be made, what would you cut instead?

- Do you think there is a way to look at art?

- Go to a local art museum. Spend the afternoon. Have a good time. Write about what you take away from the experience at the end of the day.

- Even bad art is better than no art. Respond.

- Did anything else about this essay remind you of your own experiences? In your notebook, jot down one memory, thought or opinion that popped into your head as you were reading.

One of a Kind

The devastating death of Robin Williams has made me think about the nature of genius.

When the news broke, the tributes poured in. "One of a kind! One in a million! On another plane! Nothing like him. Anywhere. Ever!"

Columnist and radio personality Colin McEnroe, in an article for *Salon,* describes Williams' standup comedy as "adrenalized" and says that he unleashed "so many personalities that 10,000 Maniacs seems an understatement."

McEnroe says of Williams, "There was just one human being who could do this thing."

Just one.

One in a million. One of a kind. Nothing like him. Anywhere. Ever.

We talk about this as if it were a good thing. But if you were the one off on another plane, if you were the *only one* who could do a thing, the *only one* of a kind in the whole world, if you were one in a million, a billion, a gazillion, where would you really be?

Alone.

Humans are a naturally gregarious species. We understand that there is not only safety in numbers, but also comfort, acceptance, belonging, love. We are happiest when we are with others who "get" us. We want to fit. It is as much a necessity of a life of quality as eating and breathing.

And, sometimes negotiating life is hard. We need advice from others who know, truly know, what our options are. But in order for all of that to happen, we need to find others who are like us. How does that happen for someone who exists on another plane?

I started thinking about this one day when I was listening to Mozart. There are three things about this great composer and his genius that strike me. First, Mozart was only thirty-five when he died, making his accomplishments that much more singular. Second, he was a child prodigy, a true genius who did what he did mostly because he couldn't help it. And finally, his genius had an unsettling effect on others. People either wrote him off as a freak or they exploited him for his weaknesses or they worshipped him for his ability or they resented him for his success. There were certainly people in his life who loved him. But no one in his sphere was his equal. No one understood him. No one.

Mozart did not take his own life, but he didn't take particularly good care of it, either. I wonder if there was anyone who could sit him down and say, "Listen, Wolfgang. I've been in your shoes and here's what worked for me." I doubt it. He was, it seems to me, at the mercy of his genius. Every day was an experiment.

That seems to be the way it is for our most creative people. Their minds inhabit a place that the rest of us have never experienced. So when they get tangled up in it, we can't help them.

McEnroe wonders of Williams, "Who knows what it was like to be that guy?"

I wonder, too.

I have a little bit of experience with the frustrations of being one of a kind. Not that I am a genius of any sort—not even close. But, as a high school English teacher, I spent most of my adult life as the smartest person in the room—the oldest, the most experienced, the most educated. The different one. I understood things about the fifteen year olds in my classroom that they would never understand about me or even themselves—at least not during the time we would be working together. It took me a while to realize, even though they seemed like rational beings (well, most of them, anyway), that they didn't see even the simplest concepts from my point of view. They couldn't. It was a physical impossibility. Their brains were not as evolved as mine, not because I was brilliant but simply because I had been alive longer. The distance between us was palpable.

So, because I was the one who could see this, I was the one who had to make the adjustments. Once I figured out ways to close the gap, I could teach them. But that didn't make us closer. I could never ask them for advice. And while we could be friendly, we could never be friends. And I could never let them know how insecure and how frustrated I felt inside so much of the time when I was working so hard to win their respect by selling myself as someone who was confident and in charge. When a teacher is with students, there is always an image to uphold, a part to play, feelings to mask. You create a persona that your kids can understand and accept and you bury the rest. When you are with them, your guard is always up and you're always "on." It's a stressful way to spend the day.

But I had an escape. In the English teachers' workroom there were others like me. My equals. My betters. Sometimes it only took a couple of minutes in their company to realize that I was really OK, on the right track, doing the right things, a part of a team. It was the few minutes of oxygen that would allow me to jump back into the pool and hold my breath for the next forty-five minutes.

And then, of course, at the end of the day, I could go home to my family and be something completely different. Me. Finally. Phew. Leave the mask at the door. Recharge. Get ready to face the next day.

But imagine this. You are fifty and *everyone* else in your life is fifteen. Everyone. Always. That means that there is always a part of yourself that you can't reveal, or, if you do, no one gets it. It's like you're Windows 10 and everyone else has peaked at Windows 7. You can read them, but, without an upgrade, they can't read you.

And when people don't get things, they tend to trivialize them. After all, if I don't get it, it can't be that important right? Kids will say, "This is sooooo stupid. Why do I have to know this?" It's not because they're mean. It's because at this point in their lives they are intellectually incapable of seeing things the way you do. So you adjust to minimize their frustration and try again. But if you don't hurry up and find some equals to validate *you*, to remind you that who you are and what you do really *are* important, you begin to feel disconnected. Irreparably different. And very much alone. Maybe not outwardly, but deep down, in that place that you've learned to keep hidden from ordinary people. And you assume the mask permanently, you give the world what they want, you stay "on" when what you need more than anything is for someone to understand what's going on when you are "off."

If you are one of a kind, you have no equals. If you have no equals, the validation that keeps the rest of us going is not available to you. You are truly peerless. It is a word that we use as a compliment. But it's not. It's more like being sentenced to a lifetime of solitary confinement.

No wonder many true geniuses have trouble negotiating life. They live in a realm of the extraordinary. And there are so very few of them. Figures on the Mensa.org website show that the IQ scores of most humans fall within one standard deviation of the mean, that 68% of people have IQs between 85 and 115. That's average. More significant is that 98% fall within two standard deviations of the mean, between 70 and 130. But, for the most exceptional among us, there are still *five more categories* on the scale—moderately gifted, highly gifted, exceptionally gifted and profoundly gifted. Scores over 200 are categorized as "unmeasurable genius."

So, even if you are just moderately gifted, your peers and betters are a scant 2% of the population. This means that 98% of all humanity will never completely understand you.

No wonder many geniuses are so fragile. No wonder many of them deal with substance abuse and addiction. No wonder many of them feel different and uncomfortable in the company of others. They are often victims of our ignorance as we either deify or crucify them. We hold them up to impossible standards and forget that they are human. To them, we may be little more than Yahoos, unreachable, stupid and cruel. But we are all they've got.

People say that Robin Williams had a mind like no other,

that he was a genius. If that's true, imagine what a burden it must be to have something that no one else has and to have to carry it alone. Always. Without relief. Without escape.

When we talk about the death of Robin Williams, we must consider many deep and complex issues. And when we talk about the life of a genius, we must always consider the terrible aloneness that comes with being one of a kind.

Robin Williams
1951-2014

Saving *Your* Life

- Write about your favorite Robin Williams roles or performances and their effect on you.

- How would you explain Williams' genius to someone who has never seen him perform?

- If you were in charge of preserving the essence of Williams' legacy, what movies of his would you save first? Explain why.

- Have you ever been unkind to someone who didn't quite fit in? Write about the circumstances as you saw them then and as you see them now.

- Do you know your IQ? Has this knowledge (or lack of it) made an impact on how you see yourself?

- How do you feel in the presence of people who are noticeably smarter than you are?

- How do you feel in the presence of people who are not as smart as you are?

- Describe a time when you tried to explain something to someone who just didn't get it.

- Write about a time when you were the big winner, the teacher's pet, the valedictorian, the fastest, the selected one, the absolute best—even if just for a moment. How did others react to you? Or, think of someone else you know who was the best—even if just for a moment. How did you feel about him or her?

- Is there anything about you that is difficult for others to understand? If so, how do you handle it?

- Describe a time that you were certain that you were in the presence of genius. What impression did it this leave on you?

- Did anything else about this essay remind you of your own experiences? In your notebook, jot down one memory, thought or opinion that popped into your head as you were reading.

Phased

The moon rose in the eastern sky, right over my neighbor's backyard, round and full. Even though the weather people threatened all week that the sky would be obscured by clouds, the evening was clear and starry. We set up some lawn chairs in the driveway and settled in to watch the show.

Several things were about to happen. The first of them was the rising of the Supermoon, the full moon that occurs when the moon swings the closest to earth as it orbits around us. According to Space.com, since the moon's orbit is elliptical and not circular, the moon actually *is* closer to us and, as such, it appears fourteen percent larger and thirty percent brighter than normal full moons. Supermoons are also less frequent, occurring only once in every fourteen full moons. Now, all that is very nice, and it certainly warrants a look, maybe out the window. But lawn chairs in the driveway? No, not enough for that. Something else, something very, very cool was about to happen.

This particular Supermoon, aka Harvest Moon, aka Blood Moon, was about to undergo a full lunar eclipse, its first in thirty years and its last for another eighteen. Regular lunar eclipses happen a lot more often—every two and half years or so. But Supermoon eclipses are a rarity. The last one was in 1982. What was I doing then? Newly married. No kids. Grad school. Life just beginning. Jeesh. An eternity ago. The next one? 2033. I can't project that far, but the thought is haunting, just the same. These three celestial events, one in 1982, one in 2016 and one in 2033, will span most of my adult life. Nothing in space time. Nothing in historical time.

Everything in my time.

That's what made it worth the lawn chair.

The plan was to sit for a while and to go in for a while, get through to the full eclipse, take a couple of pictures and then call it a night. The longer we sat, the colder it got, so sitting through the entire thing was probably not going to happen. But as I watched the shadow of the earth creep across the face of the moon, I was struck by the enormity of the event—and its utter insignificance.

I rarely just sit and look into the night sky. Whenever I do, it makes me think about how inconsequential I am, how tiny, how powerless. Tonight was no different. Here was this Cosmic Event playing out in front of our eyes and we lined up to watch because it was a Big Deal.

To us.

But to the rest of the universe, it was little more than three tiny celestial bodies lining up and casting shadows. How many gazillions of times does this happen in the universe? Who else might be sitting in a lawn chair light years from here watching their little planet cast a shadow on their teeny, tiny, inconsequential moon? How many shadows are cast in the course of how many orbits of how many suns and moons and planets?

What could our little moon possibly mean in the grand scheme of things?

Nothing.

And everything.

As the earth began its jaunt across the moon, we oohed and aahed and took pictures. We were taken by the novelty of it and how the planets aligned, so to speak, to create perfect viewing conditions for us in the northeast. I couldn't remember the last eclipse I was able to see like this (or at all), making the evening that much more singular. But then, I did something I've never done before. I looked at the moon through binoculars and something wonderful happened. Shadows sharpened into craters and seas. Light defined itself into shades and shapes. Flatness gained contour, delineation, dimension. The moon came to life.

I gasped.

Certainly I had seen a million close-up pictures of the moon. Closer and more defined than what I was seeing now. But never, ever, had I seen it like this with my own eyes. I don't know why. It just never occurred to me to do it, I guess.

And so, now, I needed to make up for lost time.

We watched as the earth's shadow crept in from the left side of the moon, moving slowly across the old man's face in an arc. Eventually it blocked much of the sun's light, causing the moon to redden and darken like a blood-shot eye. This moon hung ominously in the sky for several minutes. I watched so intently that my muscles grew tense. At the reappearance of the first sliver of light on the left side of the moon, I gasped again. Only then did I realize that I had been holding my breath.

Now I was assured that the earth and its shadow were indeed continuing along on their appointed path and that the moon would reappear in due time. What a relief.

And all was right with the universe. At least this little speck of it. At least for now.

We stayed outside for the entire four hours of visible eclipse, running in from time to time to use the bathroom, to recharge camera batteries or to make tea. Every time I thought it might be too late or too cold to stick it out, I thought how far away 2033 was, how uncertain the future always is, how it took me my whole life to appreciate the real beauty of the moon and how every moment I spent observing this evening's marvel was a moment well spent. The conditions were perfect, right now, albeit a little cold. Nothing a jacket and another blanket couldn't remedy. How often does that happen?

To the cosmos, an event like this is so infinitesimal as to be invisible. To us, it is a reminder that we are a part of something much larger than ourselves—a point, I think, of which we need constant reminding. The fact that a Full Lunar Eclipse of a Supermoon rivets *our* attention so completely reinforces the fact that we are very small and there is so much that we don't know.

And that is all the more reason to understand our world as deeply as we can—to explore it, to observe it, to see where we fit.

So, I sat outside for four hours in the cold—contemplating the change of the seasons, lamenting the passing of time, appreciating the beauty of the natural world, marveling at the unknown—while watching our little shadow cross the face of our planet's only moon. For a little while, I looked closer and thought deeper. I forgot I was cold and how uncomfortable I was in that cheap plastic chair. I forgot that our lives are finite—and short. And, for just a second, when our planet ever-so-briefly erased the moon from the sky, I even forgot to breathe.

So, a total eclipse of a Supermoon happened. I watched it. The sun, the moon, the earth and the cosmos remain unfazed by either occurrence.

But for me, it was stellar.

Saving *Your* Life

- Write about your experiences with the cosmos—eclipses, meteor showers, Northern Lights, satellites, phases of the moon, stars, constellations, etc.

- Write about a time when you endured discomfort in order to watch something that you might never have a chance to see again. Was it worth it?

- Would you go into space if you were given the opportunity? What do you think it would be like? What would scare you? What would thrill you?

- What is there in the cosmos that you take for granted?

- What in the universe do you wonder about?

- When was the last time you sat outside in a chair at night and just looked up? If it has been a while, do it soon. Write about what you see and what it makes you think about.

- Watch a movie about space travel—*Apollo 13, Gravity, Interstellar, The Martian* and *2001: A Space Odyssey* come to mind. Imagine that you are a member of the crew on any one of these thrilling and dangerous missions. How would you fare?

- What do you think is humanity's role in the universe? If we are so tiny and insignificant, why are we here?

- Is there anyone else out there?

- Did anything else about this essay remind you of your own experiences? In your notebook, jot down one memory, thought or opinion that popped into your head as you were reading.

It's Time

Time.

We are all slaves to it. Whether we are on tight schedules or have all the free time in the world, we are controlled by the clock. It frames our very existence from first breath to last.

Throughout our lives, we struggle with time and how to deal with it.

Kids can't wait for anything ever. Ten-year-olds want to be thirteen and thirteen-year-olds are panting to be sixteen. Eighteen-year-olds want to be twenty-one and thirty-year-olds wonder what all of the fuss was about.

Working parents know better than to wish their lives away, but they are so pressed that they do it anyway. *Once we get through potty training. Not until we get a little more lopped off of the mortgage. Can't wait for this rebellious stage to pass. Will we ever get this last one through college? As soon as I finish this big project. Can we please just get through dinner?*

Grandparents wish time would slow down. Words that they used to drop casually, like *spending my time, wasting my time* and *the rest of my life*, have real meaning now.

We are obsessed with time. It controls us. It is inescapable. It is the elephant in the room, the monster under the bed, the skeleton in the closet.

In movies, literature and art, time gets traveled, warped, melted, stolen, bent, stopped, twisted in lake house mailboxes and the false bottoms of desk drawers and manipulated in every conceivable way.

In real life, time warps us.

Beautiful things exist in time and then end. You can't stop on a note if you want to hear the symphony. In order to understand the significance of the events of Act One, we must move on to Act Two. If we pause the film, we have a photograph, not a movie. We must turn the page if we are to know what will happen. We are always moving on, making memories. And even those are temporary. If we don't like it, too bad.

People say, *It's tough getting old.*

But if we do not want to grow old, then we must die young. Seems like a fairly clear choice.

We can't see time or touch it. It has no corporeal self. We can't hug it or hit it. We can't speed it up or slow it down. We can't get it back. For all of our twenty-first century technology, all we can ever really do to time is measure it as it passes us by. It doesn't matter if we use a sundial or an atomic clock, the result is the same. Time has passed and we are older.

The best we can do is to lose track of time every once in a while. Become so involved in life that we forget that it is passing. Like at the movies. I know a film is a good one when I sit through the whole thing without ever once feeling the urge to check my watch. If, at any moment, I wonder how long I've been sitting there, the spell is broken.

High school teachers never lose track of time because they are reminded every forty-five minutes or so by the sound of a bell.

Students file out as others file in. Teachers learn quickly when the schedule will allow them a moment to pee or to grab a snack. (It's always *or*—never *and*.) They carefully guard those moments.

Kids themselves constantly scream out the existence of time. Not only are they real reminders of our own lost youth, but they are always looking forward to something and counting down the days. *Three weeks till my birthday. Eight more days until my driver's test. Ninety-five days till graduation!!*

Don't wish your lives away, I say.

Oh, no. I'm not. But I just CAN'T WAIT until prom!

And all the while, I'm thinking, *Twenty-seven minutes until lunch. Three hours until dismissal. Four days until the weekend. Three months until summer vacation. Two years until retirement.*

Good grief.

We all do it, figure out how to live with time, I mean. If we don't, it gets figured out for us.

When I was teaching every day, every clock in my house was set to a different time. The alarm next to my bed was set twenty minutes ahead. The clock in my car was set ten minutes ahead. The clock on the stove was good for an extra five minutes and the mantle clock stayed at standard time all year round.

I knew each changed time, each real time and the differences between them. It helped me to stay on track and get to where I was going. My husband wondered how this could possibly make a difference. If I knew that my alarm was twenty minutes fast, how could that possibly help me to get up and out on time? I could just as easily set the alarm to go off twenty minutes early. If I knew that the clock in the car was ten minutes ahead of the actual time, how did that get me to school on time?

My answer? I have no idea. The alarm set grew from my fear of oversleeping. Because of it, I am convinced, I never overslept. When the alarm proved itself, I reset the car clock and that always gave me the nudge I needed to get going, even though I knew that it was not the right time.

But what is the right time? Is there one? The measurement of time is an arbitrary construct that we all agree on—although no one ever asked me. My manipulation of time gave me a little bit of power over it. It's true that I was manipulating the measurement of time and not time itself, but that's not my point. We all have to figure out how we are going to live with time in order to make the most of it.

When I stopped teaching, I set all the clocks back to the mutually agreed-upon time. You know, the one that everyone else uses. It was a most difficult adjustment. I have no idea why. Maybe I enjoyed jousting that windmill. But now I must face the truth.

Time doesn't wait. It can be wasted but it can't be saved. Use it or lose it.

No, dear. You DON'T have ten more minutes. You never did.

The time is now.

Saving *Your* Life

- Is it possible to make every minute count?

- What is your relationship with time?

- Think about how your relationship with time has changed as you age.

- How do you waste time?

- What do you wish you had the time to do over?

- When does time drag for you? When does it seem to move quickly? Cite specific events when you noticed this phenomenon.

- If you had it in your power to manipulate time, how would you do it?

- If you could travel in time, where would you go first?

- If you could stay active and healthy, would you want to live forever?

- What have you always wanted to do? What are you waiting for?

- Did anything else about this essay remind you of your own experiences? In your notebook, jot down one memory, thought or opinion that popped into your head as you were reading.

Afterword
I Have a Great Idea! Now What?

In Volume One of *Saving our Lives,* the Afterword gave you suggestions and exercises to help you to find, focus and zero in on those specific aspects of your life that you'd like to save. I hope that you have a nice, long list of ideas—events, people, places, opinions and stories—waiting for you.

But if writing isn't your thing, you may find that just having an idea isn't enough.

If you really want to save your life forever, but you feel you need a jumpstart, you are in the right place.

Let's get you going.

Just like any other project that seems overwhelming at first, the way to tackle a piece of writing is to break it down into manageable parts. By using the exercises in Volume One (and all of the prompts that follow the essays in both volumes) to come up with a list of topics, you have already begun this process. You can now write about yourself in bits and pieces which is a whole lot easier than starting at your birth and trying to save it all. You can't. Trying to do too much is a sure-fire path to giving up and saving nothing. Some is better than none. Satisfy yourself with that.

So now you have narrowed your life down to a series of ideas that you would like to save and you have chosen the one that you want to write about first. This is half the battle.

But now what?

At this point in the game, you need to do two things. First, you need to generate enough details to tell your story. Then you need to arrange those details in a way that makes sense to a reader.

Here are some tried and true ways to get there.

A. Generating details

1. Focus.

- One small thing. That's all you need. If you've been jotting regularly in your pocket notebook as we discussed in Volume One, you have scads of ideas. Pick one. A small one. Save *everything else* for another time.

- By now, you're good at this. That's what got you here.

2. Write freely.

- Blank pages are scary. So, fill them up—the faster the better. Freewriting is a great way to do this. Write your topic across the top of your page. Set a timer for ten minutes (or fifteen or twenty) and start. Do not, under any circumstances, stop writing until the timer goes off. Do not lift your pencil from the page or stop moving your fingers on the keys. If you need more time, set the timer again. Do not stop to think. Focus as best as you can, but if your mind takes you in another direction, let it happen. It's kind of like emptying your head on the page. If you can't think of a word, skip it. Or write a nonsense word. Or write whatever pops into your head. You'll be surprised by how much you'll generate on your topic simply by not allowing yourself to stop, even for a second. Starting is the hard part. This exercise helps you to build confidence and momentum and then to use it to figure out what you have to say. No one will see it, so you never have to worry about what you have written here. It will be writing time very well spent.

- Once you have finished, take a highlighter and mark all the details that are relevant to your topic. Add whatever new details present themselves as you do this.

- If you need more details, set your timer and do this again.

- There have been many useful books written about freewriting. If you want more information about the practice, go back to the masters with Ken Macrorie's *Telling Writing* (Heinemann, 1985) and anything by freewriting guru Peter Elbow.

3. Brainstorm

- Brainstorming is another judgment-free way to find out what you have to say about a topic. It's a lot like freewriting though not as intense. Brainstorming is fun to do with someone else, if you are up for that, but you can just as easily do it alone.

- Close your eyes for a moment and picture your person, place, event, opinion or whatever. Then spew out details as fast as you can—on paper, on a white board, on a computer screen, on a voice recorder or on whatever other device suits you. It is amazing how one detail can give rise to another one that you hadn't considered before you started the exercise. Pay no mind to order or spelling or how things look on the page. The idea is to generate details about your topic—as many as you can. Don't stop until your head is empty.

- Then look at what you've written and highlight whatever is relevant. Add whatever new details present themselves as you do this.

- If you need more details, do this again. Or, try a freewrite.

4. Try Self-Guided Imagery

- This will require a voice recorder. Set it up and be ready to press "record."

- Find a place where you will not be disturbed. Sit in a comfortable chair with your feet flat on the floor. Put on some appropriate music for background if you have some, but make sure that it is an instrumental piece. You want this to help you to find your words, not to compete with them. Quiet will work better than the wrong music.

- Press "record." Close your eyes. Take a few deep breaths to find your zone. Focus on your idea—your one small thing. Picture your person, place, event, opinion or whatever as best as you can. Keep your eyes closed and talk about what you see, what you remember, what you experienced, what you want to save. Stay awake. It might help to set a timer. Do not stop talking until you are satisfied that you have nothing more to say on your topic. If you have blank moments, do not stop talking. Repeat the last thing you said or hum or say your name until you're back on track. When you are done, open your eyes and turn off the voice recorder.

- Play back your recording and transcribe the relevant details. Add whatever else comes to you as you write. You may be surprised by how much you remembered and by details that may not have presented themselves before you did this exercise. If you need to probe your ideas further, try this again or do a freewrite.

5. Use Photographs, Souvenirs and Mementos

- If you're still struggling to find your words, you may benefit from some visual aids. Pull out a few photographs of that vacation, the blue ribbon that you won at the fair, the Christmas ornament that your kid made for you in the first grade, the cherry pie recipe in your grandmother's handwriting, the first piece of good jewelry that you ever owned or the tattered favorite book you saved from when you were a kid. Look and smell and touch and reminisce.

- *Then* freewrite or brainstorm or talk into a voice recorder, following the steps above.

6. Project into the Future

- Imagine your children or grandchildren or great-grandchildren or *their* children learning these stories directly from you. Imagine your stories still existing a hundred years from now. Imagine the influence that your words could have long after you are gone. Appreciate that your words, once written, will stay written—forever. When I feel like I want to quit, the thought of this gets my motor running in ways I can't explain. It's all the incentive I need.

Now that you have come up with enough details to get started, you need to think about how to put them together. Try some of these suggestions.

B. Organizing Your Details

1. Tell a chronological story.

- If you are new at this you may find that personal stories, events or experiences are often best told chronologically. Look at the details you have highlighted or transcribed and arrange them according to the order in which they occurred—beginning, middle, end. When you start writing your draft, you will find that other details will present themselves as you write. So it's important now, even if you feel like you don't have enough details yet, to start writing. You'll be amazed by what your brain will generate if you give it a chance.

- Remember to start with one small thing. Don't try to write about a whole vacation or every minute of the wedding. Focus on the small stories that are the most memorable—arriving at that awful motel, eating at that fabulous and much-too-expensive restaurant, watching the bride dance with her father, trying to find the perfect dress—for you, Mom, not the bride! These little stories are easy to tell, start to finish, and mean so much to the reader. Best of all, they will get your creative motor running!

2. Describe something visual.

- If you want to describe a house you lived in or your childhood bedroom or a favorite classroom or a flower garden that you planted, the best approach is to pick a starting point and work around spatially. Try to give your reader a feeling for the place by providing structure in your writing that mimics the structure of the place. A good way to do this is to imagine your own eyes scanning the place—right to left or left to right, top to bottom or bottom to top—and tell the reader what you are seeing. Pick an item like a bed or a sofa or the teacher's desk as an anchor and work around from there.

Fight the urge to reveal every single thing. Only include what the reader needs to get the feeling of the place. Be sure to include sensory details that describe colors, textures, light, sounds, smells, etc. Take someone by the hand and show them your favorite place—in words!

3. Create categories

- If you are writing an opinion piece on how you feel about sports or music or places you like to visit or candidates for the upcoming election, you might consider working in categories. In other words, separate baseball from football from basketball or jazz from rock from classical or Republicans from Democrats from Independents. This will help you to consider only one thing at a time, making it easier for you to focus and to be specific. Then, if you want, you could bring them together for the sake of comparison at the end. Or, you might find that each category becomes an essay of its own. Let it happen! Keep it small.

4. Decide what is the most important.

- If you are separating your details by categories, arrange them in your draft from the least to the most important. Save the best for last.

5. Add sensory details.

- Wherever it is appropriate, add in details that will heighten your readers' sensory experience. Help them to see, hear, smell, taste and touch with descriptions of color, sound, aroma, flavor and texture. Take the time to savor these sensory memories yourself!

6. Find a printable graphic organizer.

- If you are still struggling with bringing your details together in a way that works for you, go online and search the words *graphic organizer*. A graphic organizer is a blank chart that a writer can use as a tool to generate, arrange and organize details. There are lots of different shapes, depending on what you are writing about and what genre you are working in. You will probably know which one is right for you when you see it. (Don't discount the ones for kids. They are some of the easiest to use!) Most online organizers are free and printable. Filling one out will help you to visualize the shape of your writing and should get you over the hump. I highly recommend their use.

7. Or…

- Forget all of the above and just sit down and write. Don't get up until you are done. Sometimes, that works, too.

Now, one way or another, you are ready to save your life. You have everything you need to dig in and tell your stories.

Do it!

You can.

And you should.

Acknowledgments

Writers write to reach out, to connect, to communicate, to make a mark, to be a part of the world in which they live. Yet, to actually write, one must spend most of one's time alone. It is this central irony of the writing life that I find the most challenging. In order to understand life, the writer must participate in it. But in order to produce a piece of writing, the writer must withdraw into a small room and shut the door with work on one side of it and life on the other.

Should I write about living? Or should I live? If I spend too much time writing and not enough time living, I won't have much to say. And if I spend too much time living and not enough time writing, I'll have a lot to say but no opportunity to say it.

It's a quandary, all right.

Striking that balance between writing about life and living it is something that all authors face. And when we leave our writing behind for a while to live our lives, we realize with relief that there *are* others out there and that we are not alone.

That's why we include pages like this in our books—to thank those people who stick by us even though we spend so much of our time ignoring them.

So I'll start with my husband whose support has made my

foray into writing and publishing possible. The ultimate trip planner, he gets me out into the world in ways that I would never be able to do on my own and is the reason that many of my essays exist. He also takes care of things that I neglect, like finances and snow removal and dinner and vacuuming. His vigilance and attention to the details allow me to retreat into my little room for hours and days at a time to write my essays and make books like this one. If you like my work, you can thank him.

My kids, though grown, keep me hopping and traveling and looking at life in new ways. They are a constant source of inspiration, the reason that I started all of this in the first place. They are, after all, the ones who make my life worth saving. If you like my work, you can thank them.

My extended family and circle of friends remind me that there are people out there who care about what I do and that I should keep doing it. Their encouragement and support never wavers, even when I don't return their calls. If you like my work, you can thank them.

Patrice Fitzgerald, author, publisher and teacher, convinced me that I could make the transition from blogger to published author and showed me the way. Debbie Miles, colleague and dear friend, gave this manuscript a thorough, English teacher's going-over even though she was suffering from the aftereffects of car accident. (Did a concussion make the book better, Deb?) James at GoOnWrite.com is once again responsible for the design and layout of my lovely cover, both online and in print. And formatters Jason and Marina Anderson, way down under at Polgarus Studios, have anchored my words both online and in print with patience, professionalism and skill.

I am grateful to all of these friends who waved their magic wands over this manuscript and helped to make it the book that you hold in your hands today. If you like what you see, you can thank them.

Finally, I owe a debt of gratitude to Natalie Davanti. She knows why.

It's good to know that when I'm lost in my work, I'm really not alone at all. I just have to open the door to find you all waiting on the other side.

About the Author

D. Margaret Hoffman is a retired teacher of creative writing, expository writing, literature and film. She lives in New England where the cold winters encourage long periods of hunkering down, wrapping oneself in homemade afghans, drinking herbal tea and writing. She also whiles away the winter with a host of other retirement pastimes—among them traveling with her family, enjoying local theater, studying Italian, crocheting, choral singing and playing her spiffy new ukulele. She is a blogger and the author of the award-winning collection, *Saving Our Lives: Volume One—Essays to Inspire the Writer in YOU*. As you might expect, *Saving Our Lives: Volume Two—Essays to Release the Writer in YOU* is her second book.

Follow Hoffman's blog,
sign up for her mailing list or
send her an email at

www.dmargarethoffman.com

42951215R00184

Made in the USA
Middletown, DE
26 April 2017